"свободная культура"
ул. Пушкинская 10

Товарищество Свободной Культуры:
Картины Последнего Периода из Санкт-Петербурга, России

The Brotherhood of Free Culture:
Recent Art from St. Petersburg, Russia

Виктор Андреев / Viktor Andreev

Алексей Чистяков / Alexei Chistyakov

Марина Каверзина / Marina Kaverzina

Александр Лоцман / Aleksandr Lotsman

Евгений Орлов / Evgeny Orlov

Игорь Орлов / Igor Orlov

Светлана Цвиркунова / Svetlana Tsvirkunova

MARSH ART GALLERY
UNIVERSITY OF RICHMOND MUSEUMS

Published on the occasion of the exhibition
The Brotherhood of Free Culture: Recent Art from St. Petersburg, Russia

Marsh Art Gallery, University of Richmond Museums
October 11 to December 15, 2002

Kresge Art Museum, Michigan State University, East Lansing
January 8 to March 16, 2003

Miami University Art Museum, Oxford, Ohio
May 27 to October 16, 2003

Organized by the University of Richmond Museums, the exhibition was co-curated by Joseph C. Troncale, Associate Professor of Russian, University of Richmond, and Richard Waller, Executive Director, University of Richmond Museums. The exhibition is made possible in part with the generous support of the University of Richmond Cultural Affairs Committee.

Published by University of Richmond Museums,
Richmond, Virginia 23173 (804) 289-8276

Printed by Worth Higgins & Associates Inc., Richmond, Virginia

Cover: Evgeny Orlov (Russian, born 1952). *The Ark,* 1996,
oil on canvas, diameter 37 1/2 inches. Collection of the artist.
(cat. no. 28; cover, detail; full illustration, p. 10)

Library of Congress Control Number: 2002112856
ISBN 0-9713753-4-8

TABLE OF CONTENTS

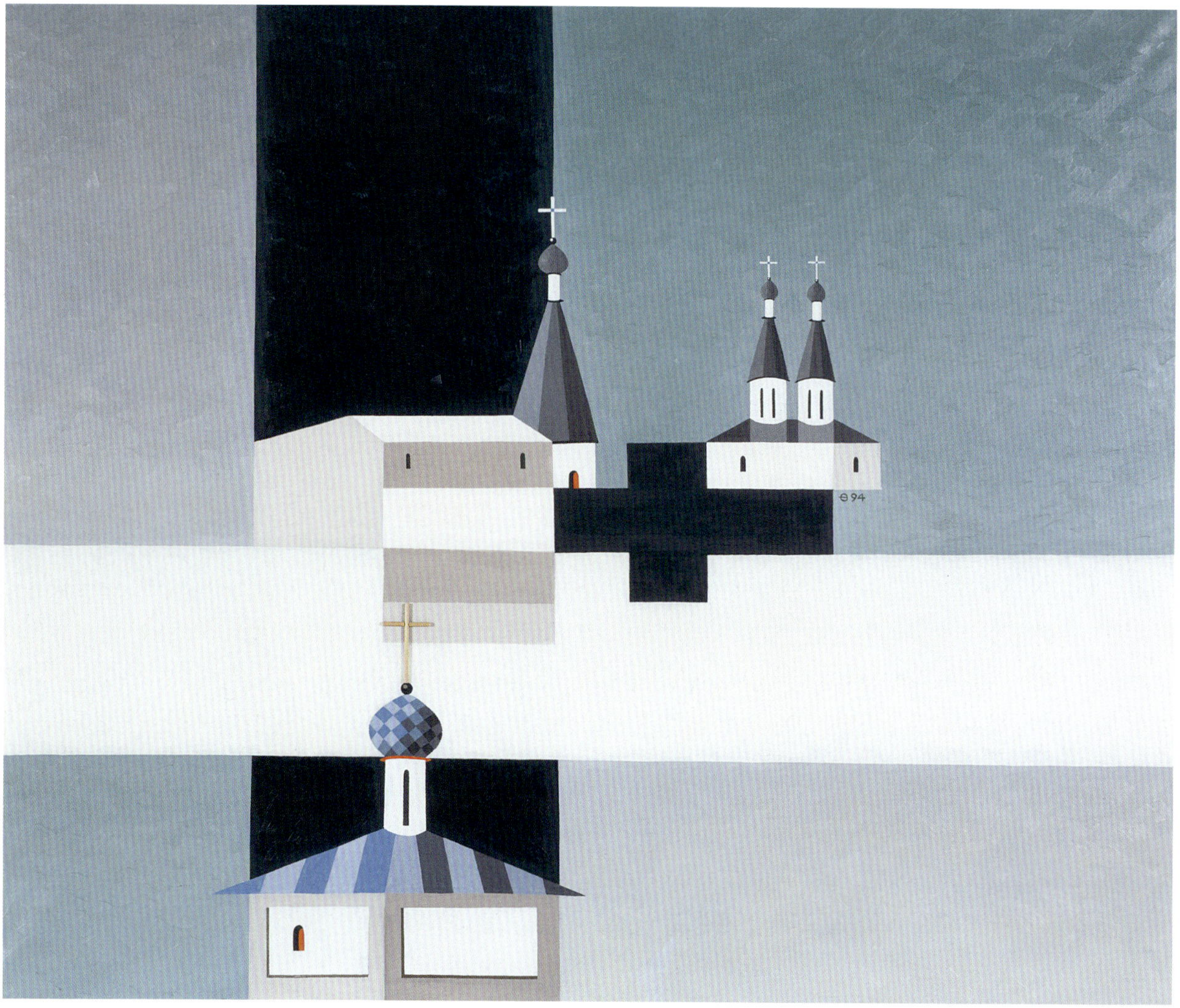

Евгений Орлов / Evgeny Orlov

Страна городов / A Country of Cities

1993, oil on canvas, 56 1/2 x 68 1/4 inches

(cat. no. 22)

DIRECTOR'S FOREWORD

We are pleased to present this exhibition of recent art from St. Petersburg, Russia, created by artists from Pushkinskaya 10. Known as the Brotherhood of Free Culture, the society was formed in 1989 as a cultural center to promote nonconformist art (often referred to as underground art during the Soviet period) in contemporary Russia. In addition to organizing exhibitions and providing performance, museum, and gallery spaces, Pushkinskaya 10 offers studio space to forty performing and visual artists at any given time. This exhibition features seven of those artists.

Heartfelt thanks are extended to all who have contributed, both directly and indirectly, to this undertaking. First, our thanks go to Joseph C. Troncale, Associate Professor of Russian, University of Richmond, who has been so helpful during the entire organization of the exhibition. Dr. Troncale initiated the idea of the exhibition, and his care and thoughtfulness throughout is sincerely appreciated.

Our deepest gratitude goes to Evgeny Orlov, one of the participating artists. He is the driving force behind Pushkinskaya 10, its many programs and activities, the "Society for Free Culture," and is director of The Museum of Nonconformist Art. We are indebted to him for all that he did in bringing this exhibition to fruition, everything from photography to shipping, from facilitating our interactions with the artists to consulting on all aspects of the project. We also thank the artists for sharing their paintings with us.

At the University of Richmond, our special appreciation goes to Dr. William E. Cooper, President; Dr. June R. Aprille, Provost and Vice President for Academic Affairs; and Dr. Andrew F. Newcomb, Dean of the School of Arts and Sciences, for their continuing guidance and support of the University Museums, comprising the Marsh Art Gallery, the Joel and Lila Harnett Print Study Center, and the Lora Robins Gallery of Design from Nature. Special thanks go to our colleagues in the Department of Art and Art History, the Office of International Education, and the Department of Modern Languages and Literatures for their support. As always, we give our appreciation to the staff of the University Museums. We also thank Teresa Hudson for her assistance.

We hope that in bringing the works of these St. Petersburg artists to America we are providing an understanding of Russian nonconformist art and an enjoyable look at the vitality of the art of today's Russia.

RICHARD WALLER

Музей нонконформистского искусства скорее всего самый молодой музей в Санкт-Петербурге, музей основанный двумя русскими художниками Сергеем Ковальским и Евгением Орловым на основе собранной ими коллекции картин художников — их друзей по неофициальным выставкам в Ленинграде в 1980 годах прошлого века.

Музей до сих пор не совсем вписывается в официальную музейную жизнь города Санкт-Петербурга своей самостоятельной и целеустремленной направленностью выставок, показывающих русское нонконформистское искусство, которое не признается официальным искусствознанием, как мощное движение в искусстве XX века и давшее огромный толчок для развития современного искусства.

Современные искусствоведы ссылаются на непонятие термина «нонконформистское» западными критиками и пытаются отнести искусство художников данного направления к разным течениям современного искусства, и в этом, как мы считаем, есть главная ошибка в оценке нонконформистского искусства.

Мы надеемся на принятие этого искусства американской публикой, которая, как нам кажется, сумеет быть выше устоявшихся мнений и попытается осознать все, что представленно на этой выставке.

Евгений Орлов

RUSSIAN NONCONFORMIST ART

The Museum of Nonconformist Art is, among other things, the youngest museum in St. Petersburg. It was founded by two Russian artists, Sergei Kovalsky and Evgeny Orlov, whose collection of paintings by their friends served as the basis for the establishment of the museum. The paintings were from unofficial exhibitions of the last century in Leningrad during the 1980s.

Even to this day The Museum of Nonconformist Art has not been entirely integrated into the official museum life of the city of St. Petersburg. This is largely due to the independent and intensely focused program of exhibitions that show Russian nonconformist art as a powerful movement in the art of the twentieth century that provided an enormous stimulus to the development of contemporary art. Official art criticism in St. Petersburg still does not recognize Russian nonconformist art.

When approaching nonconformist art, our contemporary art historians refer to the incomprehensibility of the term "nonconformist," as it is understood by Western critics. Consequently, they try to relate the art of nonconformist artists to various currents of contemporary art and, in our opinion, therein lies the main error in the present evaluation of nonconformist art.

We are confident in the reception of this art by the American public who, it seems to us, will be able to rise above preconceived notions, and will realize just what is being presented at this exhibition.

EVGENY ORLOV

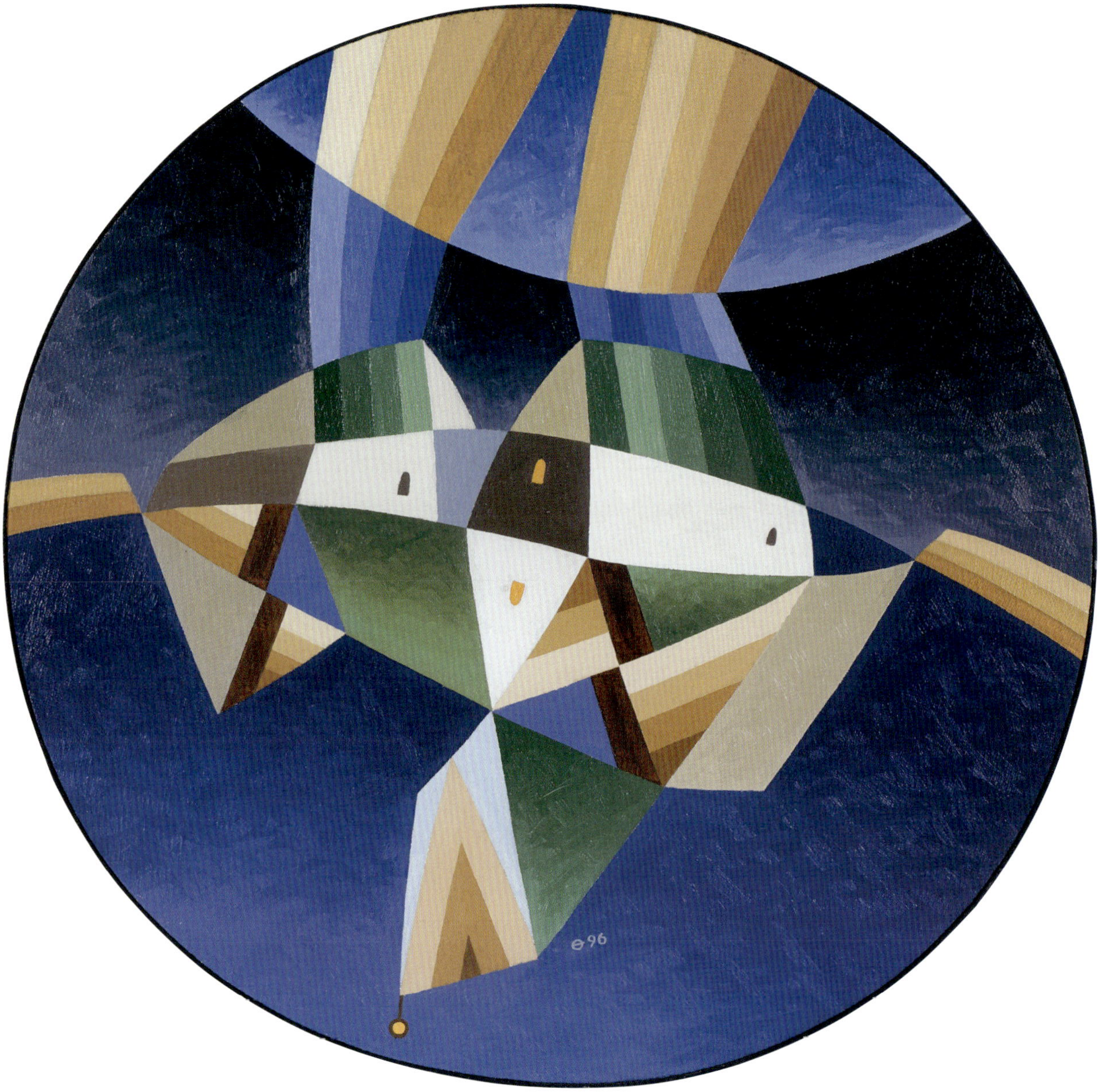

Евгений Орлов / Evgeny Orlov

Ковчег / The Ark

1996, oil on canvas, diameter of 37 1/2 inches

(cat. no. 28)

AN INTRODUCTION TO THE BROTHERHOOD OF FREE CULTURE AND THE CULTURAL CENTER OF PUSHKINSKAYA TEN

In 1863, fourteen Russian student-artists, who were about to undertake their diploma work at the Academy of Fine Arts in St. Petersburg, refused the assigned theme for their final paintings because of its rigorous and suppressive classical prescriptions. Under pressure from the liberal press and the intelligentsia of St. Petersburg as all artists were, the young students of the academy were protesting the conditions under which Russian artists of their day lived and worked.

The respect and reverence that Russian artists enjoy today became the rule only later in the nineteenth century. Until that time, within the rigid dictates of classicism, the production of all art was controlled traditionally through either imperial or ecclesial patronage. Subsequently, the young artists were expelled from the Academy and did not receive their diplomas. Instead, they formed a group known as the *Artel* and assumed the role of directing their own future as artists in direct opposition to the establishment. The action of these young artists was the initial step in the establishment of an "unofficial"[1] art in St. Petersburg that signaled the beginning of nonconformism in Russian painting. Something quite momentous had happened in that November of 1863 that would affect the course of Russian painting forever.[2]

The exhibition *The Brotherhood of Free Culture: Recent Art From St. Petersburg, Russia* represents a significant moment in the history of exhibitions of Russian nonconformism in painting. Like all Russian nonconformist art, this exhibition and these artists trace their roots back directly to 1863 and to the tradition of "unofficial" art, which, one might say, began with the refusal of those fourteen artists to remain under the yoke of the academy. The bold move of those young artists in the nineteenth century precipitated the formation of a more permanent group of painters into the Brotherhood of Traveling Art Exhibitions, or the *Peredvizhniki,* often mistakenly referred to in English as the itinerant painters. This is a misnomer. In fact, the point of the exhibitions organized by the members of that brotherhood — and a very important point at that — was not that the painters themselves would travel, but that their paintings would travel around the country, giving the population greater access to art and, in particular, to contemporary art. Interestingly enough, the majority of the population, to whom these paintings were traveling, could not afford even the four-ruble admission to see them.

From 1871 to approximately 1897 in twenty-seven major exhibitions, using the salon style of exhibitions popular in France at that time, the *Peredvizhniki* gave the world a view into the conscience of Russian artists, who were realistically portraying the problematic circumstances of ordinary peoples' lives in the hope of creating a better world for them. Running out of steam and financial backing at the beginning of the 1890s, the *Peredvizhniki* ironically rejoined forces with the academy, their avowed *bête noire,* thus again becoming a part of the establishment, in the face of which the next "unofficial" group would have to insist upon its own independent aesthetic.

Although they defected from its ranks, the *Peredvizhniki,* to be sure, had never entirely distanced themselves from the academy in aesthetic terms. It was the rigorous training that artists of the nineteenth century received at the academy that was the foundation of their extraordinary technical achievements and experimentation. In a very real sense, just as it had in nineteenth-century France, the academy played an indispensable and deeply significant role in shaping the achievements of nineteenth-century Russian painting, both technically and ideologically.

One of the most important yet often ignored parts of the history of Russian painting, particularly where "unofficial" art is concerned, is the structure of the exhibition system during any given period of history. Without some understanding of that structure, the history of Russian painting may appear more chaotic and arbitrary than it was in fact. Obviously, no form of painting can gain any measure of stature in the context of the medium as a whole, if it is not exhibited and scrutinized publicly.

At the time when "The Fourteen" made their move out of the academy in 1863, the academy and, ultimately, the imperial reach of the tsar still controlled absolutely all venues for the exhibition of painting in Russia just as it did all other aspects of Russian life. There was little, if any, possibility of "unofficial" art. This was so in a caste-like society, in which everyone fit neatly and practically irreversibly into the category either of the imperial family, of the nobility, of those who had been decorated and honored by the imperial family, of those involved in trade, or of the serfs. It was only in the liberal atmosphere created by the political and social changes decreed by the "reform tsar" Alexander II, who liberated the serfs in 1861, that it became possible to conceive of an "unofficial" art. Eventually, however, thanks to the hard-driving nationalism of the eminent publicist and art critic V. V. Stasov, the imperial support co-opted "the unofficial" realism of the *Peredvizhniki* as the official "Russian School" of painting. The realism of the nineteenth-century *Peredvizhniki* was to become the official standard of artistic form and content for a second time in the 1930s. Under Stalin, the Communist Party's rejection of the avant-garde and formalist experimentation resulted in the official elevation of the *Peredvizhniki* school as the expression of the Soviet dream through a predominant Russian socialist art.

The great movements of Western culture, such as the Renaissance, had bypassed Russia because of illiteracy and the limited production and dissemination of books.[3] This left Russia in the difficult position of having to catch up with the rest of Europe — the task that Peter the Great earnestly began in every area of Russian life at the beginning of the eighteenth century. Once Pandora's box was opened by the exhibitions of the *Peredvizhniki,* Russian painting leaped centuries ahead of itself to arrive at the point in the beginning of the twentieth century, where by 1915 it was the international leader of the avant-garde. Between 1900 and 1918, there was a blinding flurry of groups of Russian painters and exhibitions in Moscow, St. Petersburg, and abroad in Germany and France. From Sergei Diaghilev and the *Ballets Russes* and the *Miriskusniki* to the Suprematists and the Constructivists, the Russians had captured the imagination of the international art world, and, significantly, the focus of that attention was St. Petersburg, and not Moscow.

The story of nonconformism, even in such an abbreviated form as it is offered here, would be distorted without some further reference to Peter the Great and the historic cultural momentum he initiated when he decided to build St. Petersburg, sometimes called the "Venice of the North," in the middle of a swamp. Under Peter's ubiquitous direction, and much to the chagrin of Moscow — the bastion of Russian tradition — all of Russia's energies during his reign had as their focus the building of St. Petersburg as the symbol of the new Russian empire-state. Dragging Russia kicking and screaming into the modern age, Peter hacked a window to the West in the wall of Russian isolation and tradition and invited European culture to flood the country. And the torrent of ideas that poured into Russia changed her forever.

All forms of art, particularly painting, became pawns in Peter's great, mad venture. Stripped of their ecclesiastical orientation, the arts were saddled with the secular task of contributing to the building of an empire and its reputation. And it was not until those fourteen young artists protested being denied their choice of theme for the Grand Gold Medal that the force of that momentum was broken in Russian painting. Peter the Great, and Catherine the Great, had a vision of Russia's future that was inspired and directed by the idea of the individual and the merits of individuality engendered by the Enlightenment. Thus, the seeds of the rebellion of those fourteen artists in the nineteenth century, who shared that vision, were already an inherent part of Russia's development in the eighteenth century.

The cataclysmic changes in Russia after the Bolshevik Revolution had an equally dramatic effect on the direction of Russian art from 1917 to the present. In 1918 Lenin decided to make Moscow the center of Soviet power. After 206 years as the capital of Russia, now isolated, St. Petersburg was forced to bow out of the political and cultural limelight for which she was born and outfitted. Renamed Petrograd, St. Petersburg became known as a "great city with a provincial fate." The administrative command of all political, economic, social, and cultural power in Russia was then concentrated in Moscow. And, once again, as in the nineteenth century, there was no space for "unofficial" art in the ideological context of the established political regime.

What were the boundaries that separated "official" art from "unofficial" art? After a 1932 decree abolishing all artistic groups, the Party moved further towards imposing uniformity on artistic production. In 1934, after consultation with members of the artistic community, the Soviet cultural establishment adopted Socialist Realism as the official policy under which all forms of creative expression could best serve the building of socialism. The criteria for the creation of any work of art whether it be painting, film, poetry, prose, sculpture, theatre, et cetera, were *narodnost, partiinost, klassovost,* and *ideinost. Narodnost* (literally translated as "people-ness") is the quality of reflecting the essential characteristics and interests of the peoples of the Soviet Union. *Partiinost* ("party-ness") is the quality of being imbued with loyalty, dedication, service, and sensitivity to the Communist Party as the leader of the masses on the road to socialism. *Klassovost* ("class-ness") reflects the understanding of the history and principles of class warfare and the undying service to the struggle to eliminate individualism in favor of collectivism. *Ideinost* ("idea-ness") demands that any work of art must be steeped in the fundamental ideology of the Communist Party as it guides the course of the Soviet Union to its revolutionary future. Thus, the line between "official" and "unofficial" art was drawn.

Initially, the demand for adherence to these criteria was unequivocal. In the second half of the 1930s, the punishments for violation were draconian. The nation's creative genius was decimated; the names of an entire generation of creative artists were erased. During World War II, when the USSR was in a life and death struggle against an outside enemy, there was a reprieve for the alleged internal enemies of the state, among whom were those artists and writers who did not follow the course prescribed for them by the Communist Party. Once Hitler was defeated, however, the Communist Party began to tighten the screws once again within the country to ward off the ill effects of what it labeled "decadent bourgeois Western influences."

Many artists took great risks by simply presuming they were free to create. The Party defined this freedom as defiance, and, thus, illegal. From the artists' point of view, however, the creation of a nonconformist art was not necessarily their intention, but was, rather, a figment of the party's collective paranoid imagination. Thus, nonconformist art was, in effect, the party's own creation. One of the earliest postwar groups of nonconformists in Leningrad (as St. Petersburg had been renamed after Lenin's death in 1924) was the Association of Impoverished Painters (ONZh), or the *Arefiev* group that included Aleksandr Arefiev, Rikhard Vasmi, Valentin Gromov, Vladimir Shagin, and Sholom Shvarts. Their work often portrayed as utterly depressing the abject poverty of everyday existence in the Soviet Union.

Finally, after Stalin's death in 1953, ripples from the thaw in the Stalinist legacy of Soviet Socialist Realism began to make themselves felt in Moscow. Communist Party leaders and ideologues were criticizing the excesses of Stalinism and expressed dissatisfaction with the direction that the art of Socialist Realism had taken. It had become uninteresting. The ripples turned into waves of "unofficial" art that were fed by de-Stalinization. In a crucial series of stunning exhibitions in the 1960s and 1970s, "unofficial" art began to occupy an official "unofficial" position. Denied public exhibition space, "unofficial" artists in Moscow and Leningrad began to exhibit their paintings in the open air. At first, the dialogue between the ideologues and the artists begun in Moscow was only dimly mirrored in Leningrad. The city was so far away from the international scrutiny and political pressure focused on Moscow that it was more of an uphill struggle for the "unofficial" artists there to find space for their work to breathe.

The few successes during the Khrushchev era were followed by Brezhnev's crackdown on "unofficial" artists, even after a rehabilitation in 1964 of the Russian avant-garde of the 1910s and 1920s. The "unofficial" art movement gained the most ground between 1974 and 1976, when the conservative wing of the Communist Party was willing to do anything to rescue its reputation and save its political program from the ash-heap of history. After brutal government reprisals, the artists moved their exhibitions into their apartments. And it was at this time in the early 1970s that the St. Petersburg spirit came into its own again.

The authorities then began to consider nonconformist, "unofficial," or "underground" art as an anti-Soviet political movement. This official opposition helped forge a more unified coalition between Moscow and Leningrad "unofficial" artists than might otherwise have emerged. A group of nonconformist artists from Leningrad exhibited side by side with their comrades in Moscow at the *First Autumn Open-Air Exhibition* of "unofficial" art on September 15, 1974. Commonly known as "The Bulldozer Incident," the exhibition of the work of thirteen courageous artists lasted for two hours before the authorities bulldozed it. Several paintings were destroyed in the mayhem, and, along with some of the artists, members of the foreign press were manhandled by agents of the KGB. The international outcry following the reports of what happened forced authorities to issue a permit for the *Second Autumn Open-Air Exhibition* two weeks later. Lasting from noon to 4 P.M. on September 29, the exhibition of sixty "unofficial" artists at a park in the Moscow suburb of Izmailovo was attended by more than ten thousand people.

On the heels of this victory and after several other successful indoor exhibitions, in 1976 the "Brotherhood of Experimental Exhibitions" (TEE) was formed in Leningrad to unify all nonconformist artists in their efforts to hold exhibitions of each other's work and to organize related events promoting such activities. However, pressure from the authorities continued to mount, and the victory was short-lived. Nonetheless, exhibitions in apartments continued to attract as many as two thousand people over a four-day period despite harassment and threats of arrest. The work begun by TEE was continued in the 1980s by another organization known as the "Brotherhood of Experimental Visual Art" (TEII). As many of Leningrad's nonconformists emigrated, an "artist drain" was created. Given the continuing dire economic circumstances in which an artist must struggle to survive, this drain continues to plague today's Russia.

Organized in the 1990s, the "Brotherhood of Free Culture" (TSK) is the living link in St. Petersburg to the history of nonconformist art in Russia that continues the struggle to create opportunities for the free and open expression and exhibition of art unconstrained by politics or commerce. At the end of the 1990s, in order to preserve the cultural and artistic traditions of St. Petersburg and to maintain the links with the past generations of Soviet and post-Soviet artists, Evgeny Orlov and Sergei Kovalsky, veterans of the movement of "unofficial" artists and organizers of the "Brotherhood of Free Culture," conceived and established The Museum of Nonconformist Art at "Pushkinskaya Ten" (House #10 on Pushkin Street). In the experience of Russian culture, it is a unique occurrence to witness such a success of the initiative of creative people, who, during the Soviet period, had represented "unofficial" art and, subsequently, had developed the idea of "a place of its own in the Motherland."[4] The museum has an archive of the history of nonconformist art and houses a collection of artistic works of the second half of the twentieth century, and it provides St. Petersburg and the international community with a regular program of exhibitions. The University of Richmond Museums' exhibition from St. Petersburg's Museum of Nonconformist Art presents to the American public, for the first time, the most recent phase of Russian "unofficial" art from the last decade of the twentieth century and the first decade of the twenty-first century.

There is no doubt that the seven artists participating in this exhibition would each offer distinct definitions of his or her own role in the tradition of Russian nonconformist painting and would each understand the meaning of nonconformist painting differently. While the works speak for themselves, clearly and boldly embodying the artists' different attitudes, a brief consideration of just what nonconformist art may mean in the Russian context seems appropriate.

It has been said that the primary activity of human beings is the effort to exceed or transcend the dilemma of human existence.[5] Many would argue that, instead, the primary activity of human beings is to give meaning to human existence. Entertaining both for the moment as primary activities of our species, it seems useful to consider how well we have done either in the century we have just left behind. For example, beginning with the Russian Revolution of 1905 and the Bolshevik Revolution of 1917 and ending with the devolution of Marxism into the stagnation of Soviet Socialist reality of the 1980s, history might consider Russia the greatest monument of the past century to humankind's most ambitious attempt and failure in both categories. Both the attempt and failure represent humankind's apparent collective inability to grasp the nature of conditionality or of the ephemerality of all aspects of conditional, mortal existence itself as being inherently incomplete and unsatisfactory, and indifferently so.

Nonconformism may be understood to be an inherent reaction of the human psyche to the restrictions that mortality and mortal existence place on being. "Man's suffering lies in his presumption that there is a difference between Being and Form, between Consciousness and Energy, between Moveless Being and the world of appearances."[6] This classic imagined separation or difference puzzled Socrates as the question of the separation of body and soul. Rousseau pinpointed as a turning point in civilization man's alienation from himself in his felt need to feign appearances different from his being to win the approval of his peers. The Tao represents all of reality as only "is" to confound the "not this / not that" which represents the binary logic of man's ratiocination. Nietzsche critically explores ressentiment and the subsequent creation of an ascetic ideal that precludes the possibility of truly uncompromised being and life in human form. In Freud's theory of the personality, the ego is the mediator between the self and the world, other individuals, and even one's own body — the ultimate example of the obsessive fear we have of form.

Out of their own individual cultural experiences, artists of the twentieth century defined the dilemma of human existence in terms of form — cast as the very limitations of being human. The forms themselves, in which being manifests itself, appear to be our own nemesis. The conditionality of human existence, our mortality, and the absolute lack of power to control our or anyone else's appearance or disappearance from this conditional realm have backed us into a corner revealing our impotence. Yet, Rousseau, Nietzsche, and Freud tell us how we cling to form as if that were all that we are. Yet form, or, at least, our misperception of its function and what it is, seems to have always betrayed us at every turn. One has only to visit Treblinka, Auschwitz, or Babi Yar to feel the mood of betrayal, in which the past century still smolders in our memory. The dilemma we have made, then, seems, paradoxically, to be our unwavering inclination to trust absolutely in form and in the conditional realm that we inhabit. Our activity of dilemma robs us of the vision of the unconditional or spiritual realm as the ineluctable companion to our inescapable lot as form and conditionality.

Russian painters of the twentieth century have made their own unique investigation into the dilemma of human existence and how to come to terms with it. Some have fragmented form, breaking it down and reconstituting it in ways that present an often disconcerting vision of the conditionality of existence. Others have tried to go "beyond" form, attempting in the very creation of new forms to somehow trick form into denying itself. None, however, have gone so far as to renounce the possibility of embodying their vision of meaning — a non-conditional reality.

Thinkers after Plato have focused on the suffering that results when human beings subjugate themselves to illusory forms of mortal existence. Deeply rooted in the neoplatonic spiritual tradition of Eastern Orthodoxy, Russian artists have tended to view aesthetic activity as an involvement in the struggle to move beyond an illusory world of appearances and to unite with unchanging non-material being. Perhaps nonconformist art in Russia, like all expressions of nonconformism, does indeed express first and foremost the reaction of the human psyche to the restrictions that mortal existence apparently places on being.

Although it is true in some cases, it would be a mistake to assume that all nonconformist art in Russia, or in the former Soviet Union, is or was a political statement in the narrowest sense of the word. To reduce it to a political statement would be to deny its virtues as art. Ironically, it may be true that Russian nonconformist artists merely accepted the role that the party assigned to them. Russian "nonconformist art," the description that "unofficial" Russian artists applied to their work from the mid-1970s on, is an expression of inherent human freedom that is indifferent to politics. Rikhard Vasmi, one of the leading nonconformist artists after World War II, said: "The fact that I was never allowed to call myself officially an artist had a very positive influence on my development. The less official one's life is, the more personal freedom one has."[7] Russian nonconformist artists assume a position that transcends the arena of petty political maneuvering. Traditionally this is the position held by all truly great Russian artists. Pushkin (1799-1836), Dostoevsky (1821-1881), Tolstoy (1828-1910), Mandelshstam (1891-1938), Pasternak (1890-1960), and Solzhenitsyn (born 1918), to name but a few, did not equivocate or compromise their vision by turning it into a challenge to political structures or ideologies. Their role was simply to articulate the truth; that was challenge enough. They did not calculate the consequences that are essentially political. Russian artists consider it their mission to serve as the conscience of their people. They are compelled to create without assessing the cost.

Today in Russia, nonconformist art still represents the moral imperative of artists to teach or lead the way and to maintain the integrity of the aesthetic process against pollution or dilution by any outside influences. This does not mean, however, that Russian nonconformist art is purely art for the sake of art. The didactic tendentiousness of Russian art is part of the nature of the beast. However, the Russian nonconformist artist tirelessly insists on his or her unequivocal right to hold fast to an individual point of view, no matter how far it diverges from all other views and stances, and even because it diverges from them. As Russian artists bask in a newly found and still tenuous freedom, where the market rather than the state determines who survives, nonconformist art, now no longer underground, has taken flight in remarkable ways. Now unfettered, the artists have been trying their wings beyond what was even imaginable to them a decade or so ago.

The five men and two women, represented in *The Brotherhood of Free Culture: Recent Art from St. Petersburg, Russia,* constitute a widely diverse group, whose common experience includes years of working under the constraints of the Soviet system. Some even served prison sentences for various expressions of their nonconformism that have not always been artistic. The constraints they face today are different, and different, too, is the impact made by their work in today's context.

As is evident in the paintings in this exhibition, nonconformist art is not necessarily synonymous with abstract art. Created in the last decade of the twentieth century, the works range from futurist acrylic patterns and studies in texture and color to paper and cloth collages and nondimensional architectonic figures.

Evgeny Orlov, the paterfamilias of Pushkinskaya Ten, has been and still is a peripatetic and conspicuously active leader in the avant-garde culture of St. Petersburg. Much of what has transpired at Pushkin Ten is due to Orlov's unflagging efforts as one of its directors to save the best of a culture he fears is in danger of extinction. Orlov's images reveal something about both the artist and his world. One can sense the harmonic resonance of the images in Orlov's paintings with the artist's inner sense of himself and his understanding and perception of the world around him. The sparse detail in all of his landscapes reflects the simplicity of his worldview. "Dispensing with superfluous detail," he says, "is akin to the purification of the soul."[8]

Orlov privileges the dissolution of dimensional constructs in his work. In his canvases, objects do not exist as closed systems of forms or as static categories of mind and thought, but are, rather, manifestations of the inherent harmony and unity of the universe, indifferent to the imposition of space or time and conventionality. The fluid relationship in his works between architecture, its natural surroundings, and images of water is a blend of traditional Russian and Eastern associations. In a kind of magical playfulness, Orlov defuses form of the profound seriousness that humankind invests in the rigid structures of order and dimensionality. His principle of creativity may be called a kind of spiritual aerodynamics by which change is seen, not as a threat to the security of habituated creatures, but as necessary to the full evolution of the universe. In so far as art, such as Orlov's, convinces humankind of the later, beauty will save the world, as Dostoevsky is often thought to have said.

The vision that his paintings reveal combines his simple love and strong affinity for the sea, or for water in general, with a metaphysical, spiritual affinity for water as the element and "source of being" in which all of reality is engulfed, floats, and has its being. Had he been born in Moscow, perhaps, he would have had a different vision. While St. Petersburg's water-world of lakes, rivers, and canals symbolizes the superstitious and fantastic dreamlike miasma out of which the city itself was born in the mind of Peter the Great, the water-world of the Russian north is the wellspring of the mystical in the Russian soul. The Russian north — Valaam, Kizhi, the Volkhov and Svirsky regions — is the land of spiritual pilgrimage for Russians and the heart of the great mystical vision of Russia's saints. Together with Staraya Ladoga, all are situated in the marine worlds of rivers, seas, and lakes. The physical environment of these areas, the dominant feature of which is water, is represented as a key to and as the embodiment of the understanding and living of the life on the "other side" in infinity. Included among Orlov's work in this exhibition are three paintings of these mystical places: *On the Islands* (cat. no. 30), *Visions of Volkhov* (cat. no. 24) and *Old Ladoga* (cat. no. 26).

In the first painting, *On the Islands*, it seems as if from a bird's-eye-view we are suspended with the islands in the water-world of the Russian north as they rise and even take their form from the cool pastel blues. The islands in the background lose themselves completely in the blues of this living water that is the source of their spiritual significance and attractiveness to Russians. The islands reach upward and forward as beacons, finally appearing in our conditional realm in the foreground as the beige and brown chapel of one of Russia's hermits, who formed the backbone of Russian spirituality.

The other two paintings, *Visions of Volkhov* and *Old Ladoga*, resemble each other in composition and color. Old Ladoga is located in the Volkhov region in northwestern Russia's Leningrad Oblast, and both are closely connected by their historical significance in the founding of Russia. The color schemes in both paintings are practically identical. The water-world in which the apparent structures float and from which they draw their own colors sustains the structures at the junction of its graduated scale of grayish to dark violet-blue. The structures would be somber and mute, but for the thin rectangular windows in each from which a golden orange light shines, portending the warmth of human presence. Each painting has a church that seems to be stably moored in the water-world from which it springs.

These paintings transport us to a land that is transformed by the artist's love and sense of the profound significance that the region has in his own and Russia's identity and destiny. Through the power of Orlov's vision, these are spiritual, not physical, landscapes brought to life, brought into being by the water in which they inhere.

Marina Kaverzina's canvases rescue and vigorously release the explosive potential of color, sound, and rhythm from mindless convention as she wends her way through the inner landscapes and illusions of human passion and imagination. The dynamism in her work is her unfettered expression of joyful free movement and form in a sea of brilliant color. For example, she takes the traditional, sacred themes of the Trinity (cat. no. 15, illustrated p. 41) and the Crucifixion (cat. no. 11) and explores the fundamentally joyful aspects of these mysteries that sometimes have been shrouded by solemnity and left devoid of life by convention and myth.

Viktor Andreev inhabits a world where he is the sole arbiter of meaning and form. Only in his work is he free. He paints quickly to stay ahead of thought and definition. In his painting he is beyond the ordinary and the deadly monotonous reach of the recognizable. Humanity does not interest him in its current state; only man, standing free of the conditions that bind him, soaring within to a source of unlimited imagination and spiritual depth, enters the space of Andreev's tolerance. The tactile and visual luster of his canvases tantalize one to slip away into one's imagination and yield to the lure of their sensuality. He immerses us in the extremes of his palette, chilling us with his icy blues and whites, and warming us with fiery golds, oranges, and pinks as we visually cut a path, feeling securely home already, through the jagged edges of the shapes on the surface of his canvases.

The work of Igor Orlov plays in the nether world between articulation and thought. The artist focuses not on the depiction of finality in images, but on the process of their evolution where the primal energies of creativity brood and boil before exploding into form and convention. Extracting essence from the primeval bilge of human confusion, he choreographs powerful canvases of ambiance and ambivalence. We see raw emotion before it becomes channeled into fear, anger, hate, or love. In *Composition with Two Figures* (cat. no. 34) and *Untitled* (cat. no. 36, illustrated p. 59), we see the darkness of that untapped world as it ignites and fires the imagination. As the shadows of form begin to emerge, they are frozen in place forever. Orlov's paintings are unspoken passion longing for finality. In *We Drank Spanish Wine All Night* (cat. no. 33, illustrated p. 55) and *Untitled* (cat. no. 32), we have two canvases of pure white background with figures banded with belts of roughly applied black. It is as if the figure in each painting is sealed up by the heavy bands of paint, held back from the next step of its materialization as it strides forward to emerge from the light of conceptualization.

The unique dynamic quality of Svetlana Tsvirkunova's pieces lies in her ability to evoke a profound strength of attachment to tradition while exploring its boundaries. No less serious, her investigation of those boundaries is not a slap in the face of taste. She cajoles her viewer to participate in her vision. Akin to Evgeny Orlov's paintings, Tsvirkunova's work abstracts her images from their bondage to conventionality and dimensionality. They are larger than life, pushing against the edges of her canvas. Tsvirkunova gently blends warm browns, soft beiges, and a rather neutral rust with muted whites to stay the hand of accent or insistence. To achieve harmony, she weaves the investigation of abstraction with, as she says, "just the right touch of feeling."

The world through the eyes of Aleksandr Lotsman is a tranquil abode of nature where the furies of human chaos are held at bay. Lotsman flattens the space in his paintings to create a harmony between the objects in his compositions. Nothing dominates anything else. Lotsman seems to be depicting "Being, Itself" — a natural world in which there is no depth, no complication beyond the pure satisfaction of existence. There is no primacy in being but "Being, Itself." In *Birds* (cat. no. 16, illustrated p. 43), the birds are the field and path in which they stand and the water that flows in and out of them. In *A House under a Tree* (cat. no. 19, illustrated p. 47), the tree and the pile of fruit on the table are mirror images of each other's bounty and fullness. Space for Lotsman is merely where the world of color plays off, around, in, and through different shapes.

Alexsei Chistyakov's paintings are charged with the primal energy that conducts meaning between humankind and the universe, of which we are but a particle. The very condition that man finds himself in is the discovery, not the object, of art. Chistyakov sees the role of the artist as the conduit, the medium, between humankind and the cosmic force that is at the same time the source and the condition of being. His work is an investigation of the form that eludes all form where intuition alone can be our guide. He paints a window for us on cosmic ultimacy.

Struggle has always forged a common bond between artists in Russia. They know and respect each other, and they often celebrate and commiserate together. Collectively, the artists participating in this exhibition have struggled for years against a reluctant city government to acquire and restore the space their cultural center now occupies. A metaphor for the path of those who preceded them, theirs is the story of nonconformism in Russian art. Their work represents a strength and commitment that is a way of life — a way of Russian life. They welcome this rare opportunity to share their work with us. It is exciting to imagine the form that nonconformist art of future Russian artists will take, when their experience of their motherland will be entirely different from that of the artists whose works are in this current exhibition. In this exhibition we make a significant step in knowing that Russia of the future.

JOSEPH C. TRONCALE

ENDNOTES

1. The use of the word "unofficial" within the Russian and Soviet contexts has connotations with significant historical and political nuances that go far beyond the simple use of the word in relationship to art.
2. For an excellent study of the Association of Traveling Art Exhibitions see Elizabeth Valkenier, *Russian Realist Art, The State and Society: The Peredvizhniki and their Tradition* (Ann Arbor:Ardis Press, 1977).
3. For a full discussion of this topic see the introduction in James Cracraft, *The Petrine Revolution in Russian Imagery* (Chicago: University of Chicago Press, 1997).
4. Quoted from a conversation with Sergei Kovalsky and Evgeny Orlov in June 2001.
5. From the published talk "The Primary Function of Human Existence Is the Effort to Exceed the Dilemma of Human Existence" given by Adi Da Samraj on March 10, 1998, at Da Love-Ananda Mahal, Hawaii.
6. Carolyn Lee, *The Promised God-Man is Here* (California: The Dawn Horse Press, 1999) p. 693.
7. Quoted in Alla Rosenfield and Norton T. Dodge, gen.ed., *From Gulag to Glasnost: Nonconformist Art from the Soviet Union* (New York: Thames and Hudson, 1995), p. 103.
8. Quoted from a conversation with the artist in May 1997.

Виктор Андреев
Viktor Andreev

Людям приходится много думать о свободе!, свободе духа или внутренней свободе поступков — душевных переживаний.

Эти размышления как бы ответ на монотонность повседневного существования, на предсказуемость будущего и ее обыденность.

Абстрактное искусство — эта прекрасная и доступная возможность свободно перемещаться в пространстве духовности, тут нет авторитетов и законов, все решаете только Вы в пространстве белого холста и вашего самочувствия.

Это такое «путешествие», и каждый раз оно начинается заново.

Очень демократично, толерантно и действительно абсолютно свободно в Вашем понимании.

People have to think a lot about freedom! Freedom of spirit or of the inner freedom of actions — of life's spiritual endurance.

These considerations are like a response to the monotony of daily existence, to the predictability of the future, and to that predictability's ordinariness.

Abstract art is that marvelous, available opportunity to freely move into the space of spirituality; there are no authorities or laws there. Only you decide everything in the space of a white canvas and of your own feeling.

It is just such a "journey," and every time it starts all over again.

It is very democratic, tolerant, and really absolutely free in your understanding.

Виктор Андреев / Viktor Andreev

Композиция / Composition

2001, acrylic and lacquer on canvas, 39 x 46 3/4 inches

(cat. no. 1)

24 – 25

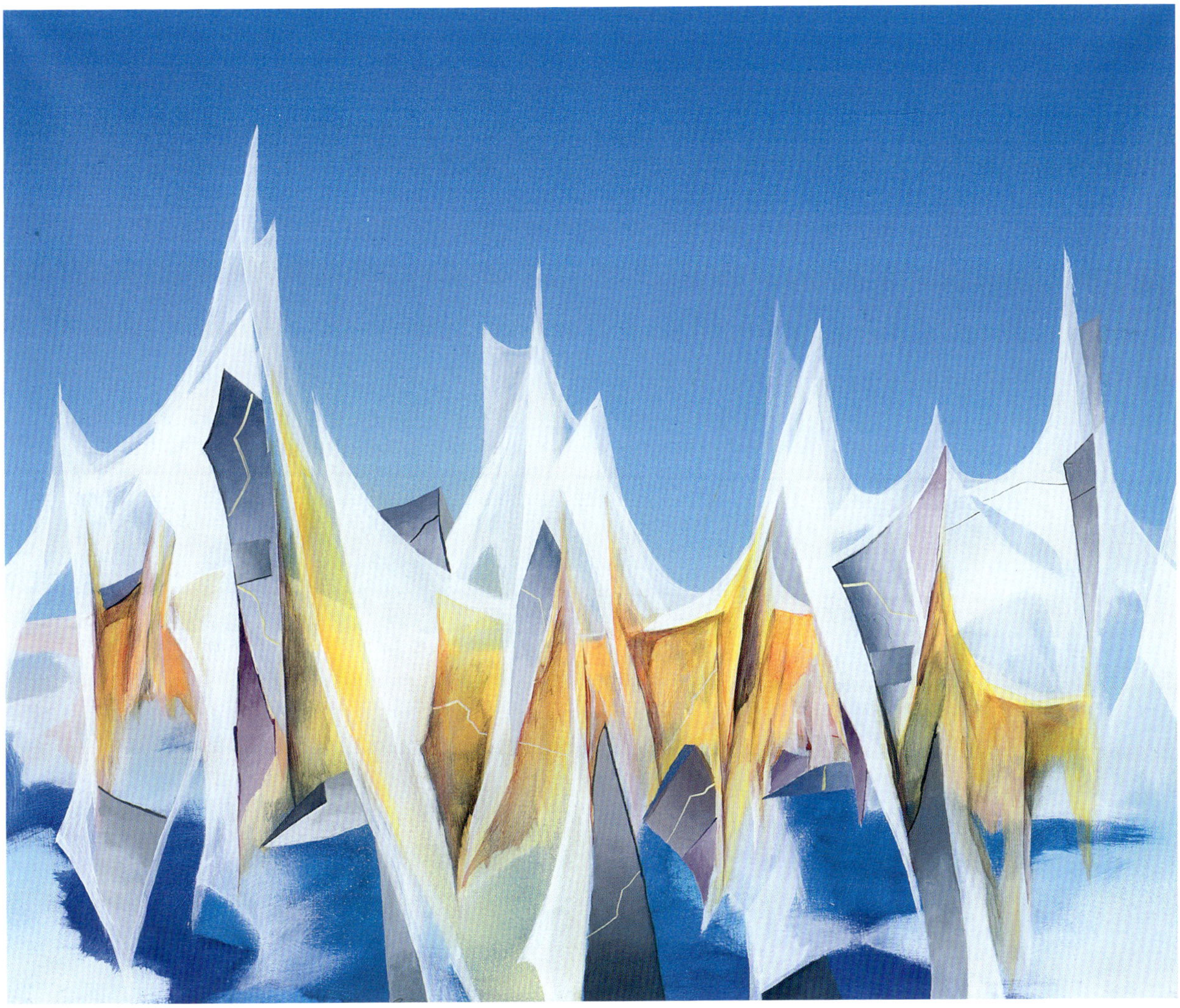

Виктор Андреев / Viktor Andreev

Композиция / Composition

2001, acrylic and lacquer on canvas, 39 x 45 inches

(cat. no. 3)

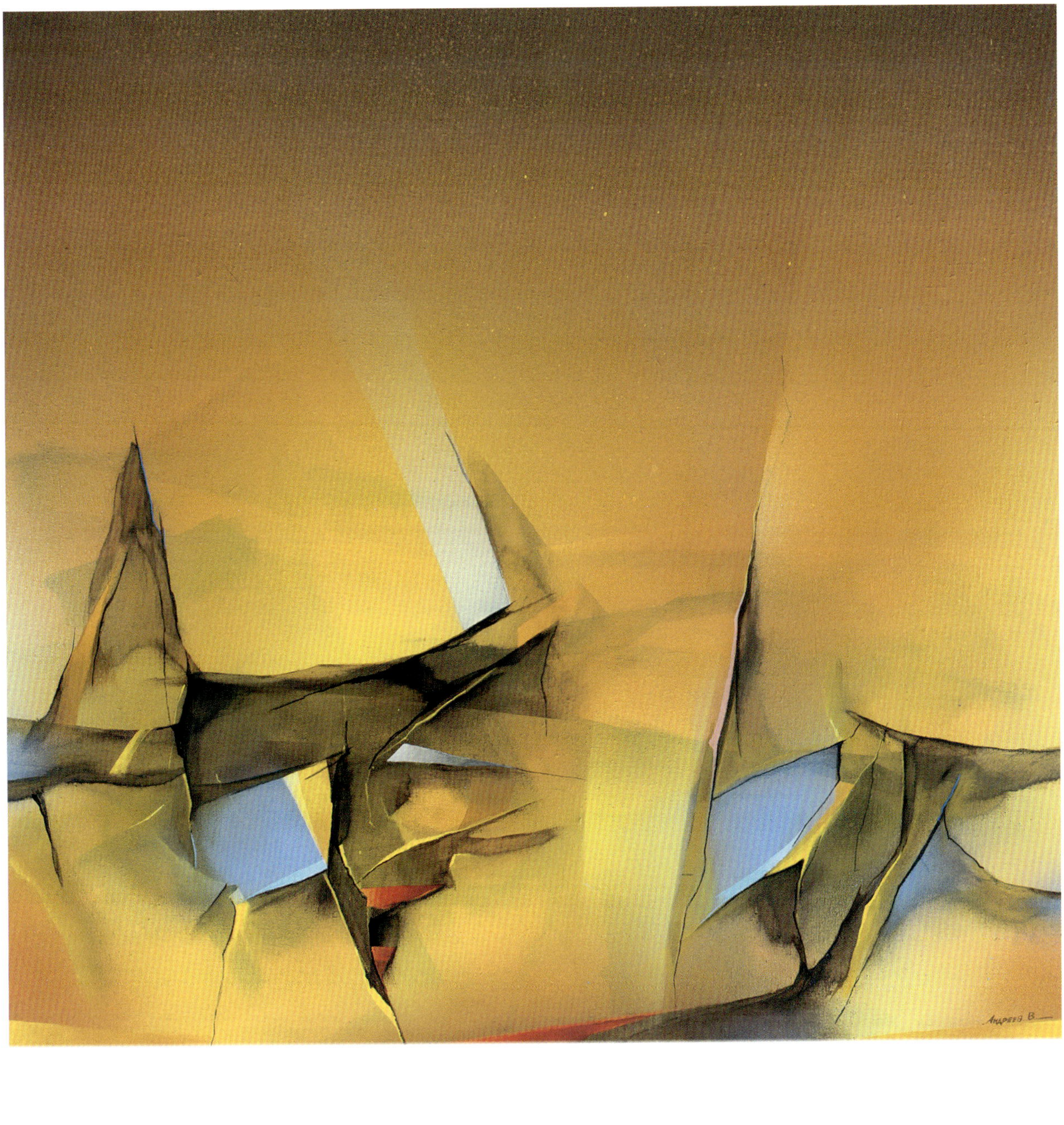

Виктор Андреев / Viktor Andreev

Композиция / Composition

2001, acrylic and lacquer on canvas, 39 x 46 3/4 inches

(cat. no. 4)

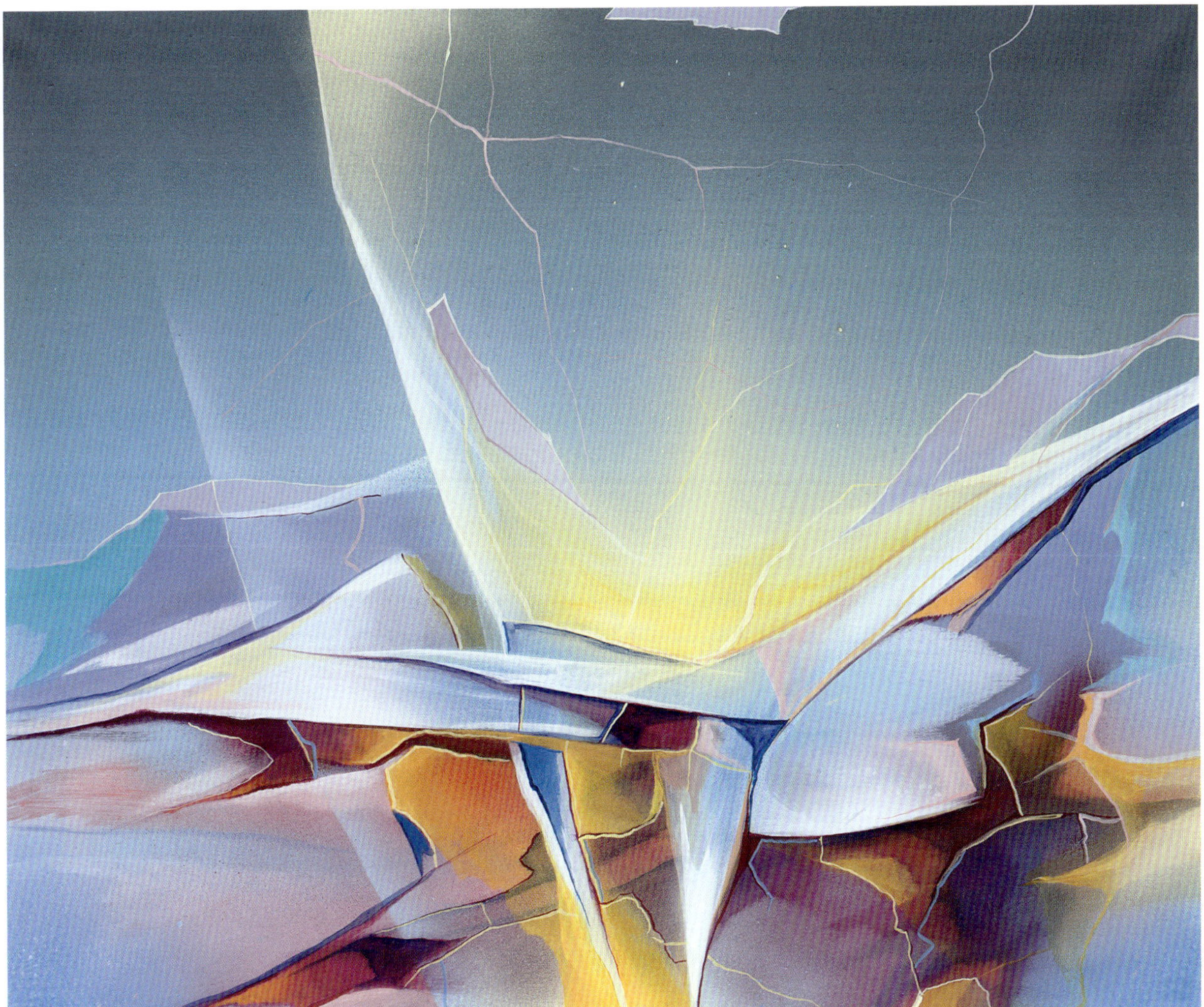

Алексей Чистяков
Alexei Chistyakov

Основным в искусстве для меня является состояние, которое передает объект искусства, в частности — картина. Энергетика, которая переходит из космоса через художника зрителю в мир.

For me the basic thing in art is the condition which an object of art conveys, specifically — a painting. The energy that moves from the cosmos into the world through an artist to the viewer.

Алексей Чистяков / Alexei Chistyakov

Без Названия / Untitled

1994-97, oil on canvas, 64 1/4 x 59 inches

(cat. no. 6)

Алексей Чистяков / Alexei Chistyakov

Без Названия / Untitled

1999, oil on canvas, 27 1/4 x 54 1/2 inches

(cat. no. 8)

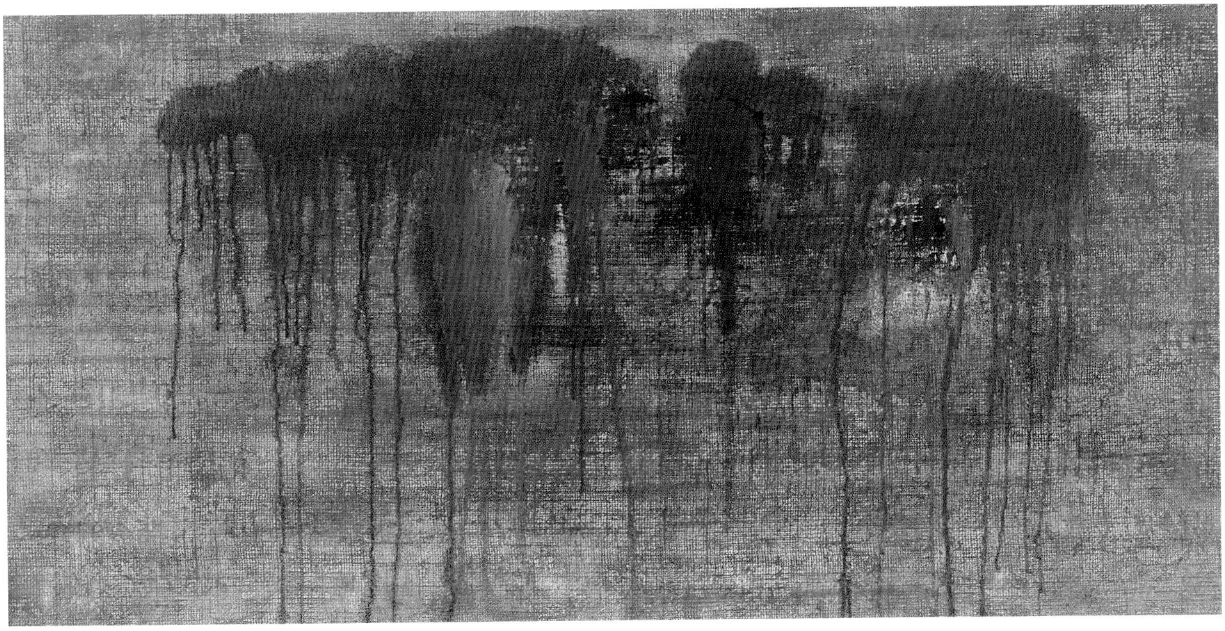

Алексей Чистяков / Alexei Chistyakov

Без Названия / Untitled

1999, oil on canvas, 55 1/2 x 36 1/4 inches

(cat. no. 9)

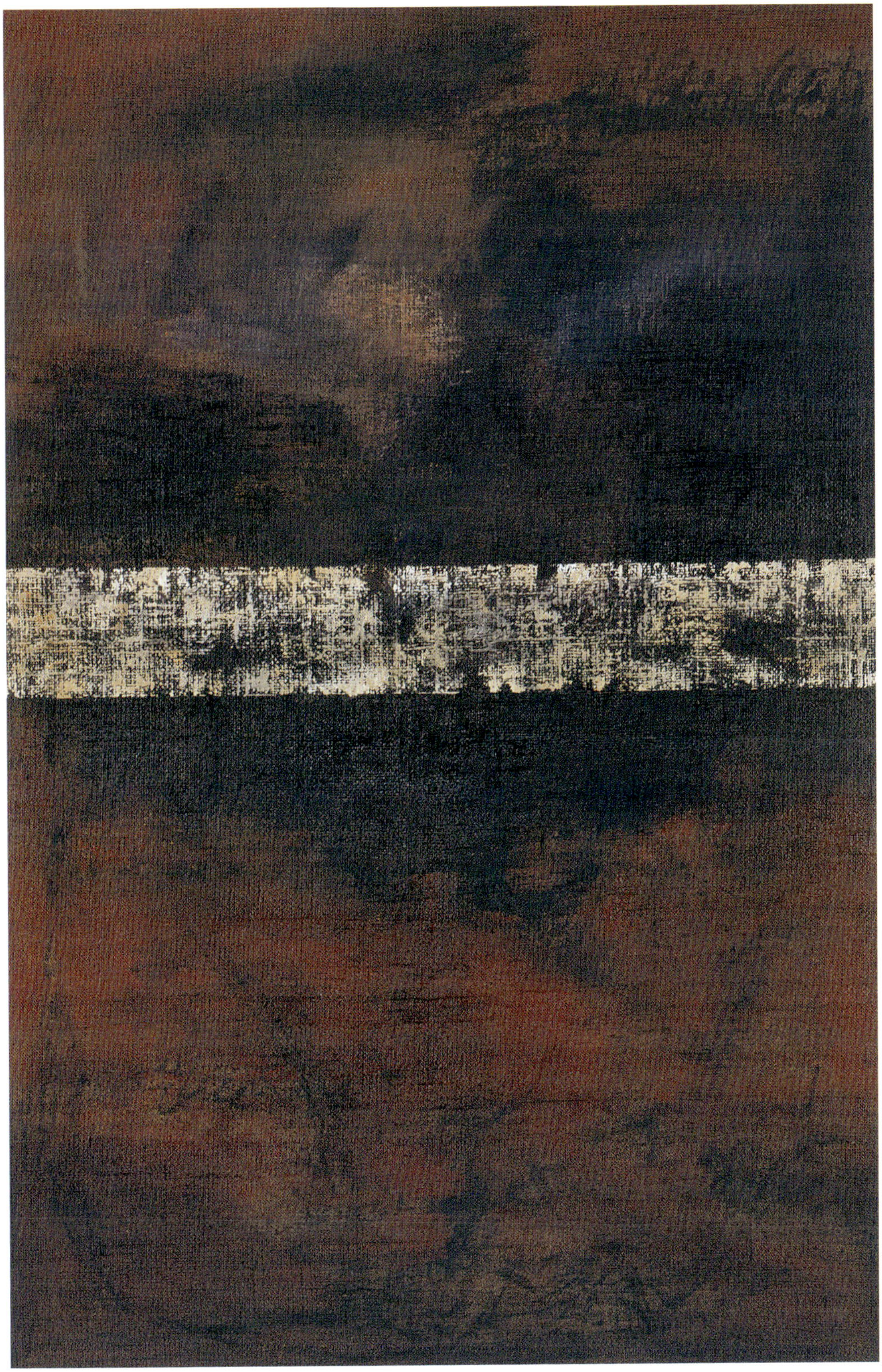

Марина Каверзина
Marina Kaverzina

Эпицентром своих живописных движений предполагаю стремление оперировать неиссякаемой потенцией заключенных в человеке энергий-стихий-страстей: цветовых, звуковых, ритмических. . .

Любимая гимнастическая позиция — «жест освобождения», рождающий в живописи радость свободного движения форм, экспрессивную динамику, иллюзию полета в легком пространстве, упоение чистой энергией цвета и бурными ударами (не тонкой кисти, а швабры, руки, пропитанной краской тряпки).

Любимая интеллектуальная позиция — «следопыт» — «прослеживание следов» образов-знаков-мифологем в созданных цветовых интерпретациях реальности.

Изобразительный язык и философско-мифологические легитимации этого языка я определяю не как остро-новаторские и оригинальные, а как авторские репортажи о путешествиях в парадоксальном и восхитительно странном лабиринте внутренних ландшафтов.

I suggest that the epicenter of my artistic movement is the aspiration to unleash the inexhaustible potential of the energies, elements, and passions locked up in humankind that are colorful, sonorous, rhythmical. . .

My favorite gymnastic position is the "gesture of liberation," which by furious strokes (not of the palette, but of a broom, a hand, a rag soaked with paint) gives birth in a painting to the joy of the free movement of form, to expressive dynamics, to the illusion of flight in light space, and to the ecstasy of the pure energy of color.

My favorite intellectual position is that of a "pathfinder" following the trail of images-signs-mythologies in interpretations of reality made in color.

I see the graphic, depictive language of art and the philosophical and mythological legitimations of this language not as sharply innovative and original, but as an artist's reports on journeys in the paradoxical and captivatingly strange labyrinth of inner landscapes.

Марина Каверзина / Marina Kaverzina

Пианист / A Pianist

2001, oil on canvas, 54 1/2 x 46 3/4 inches

(cat. no. 12)

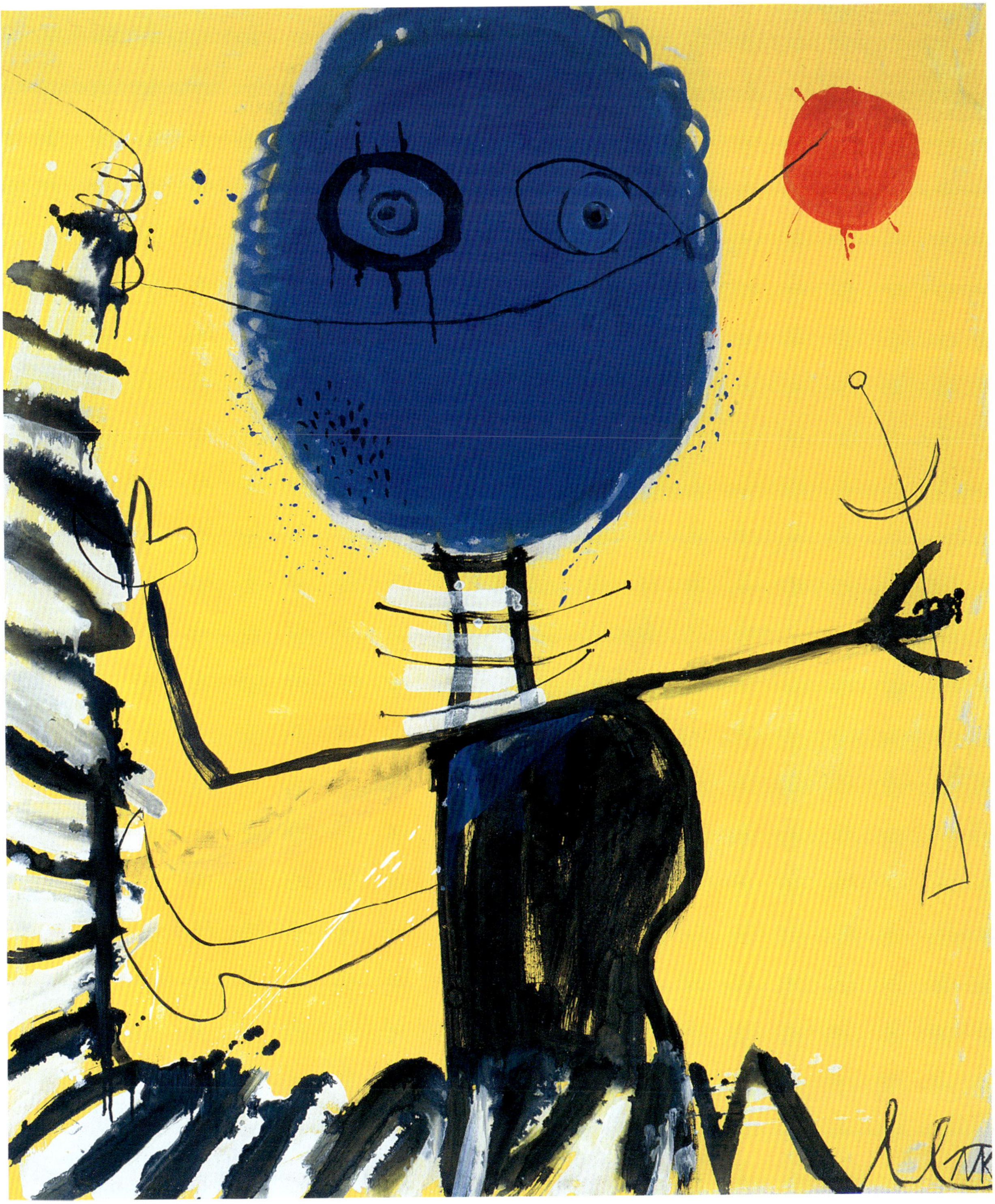

Марина Каверзина / Marina Kaverzina

Автопортрет / Self-Portrait

2001, oil on canvas, 54 1/2 x 46 3/4 inches

(cat. no. 13)

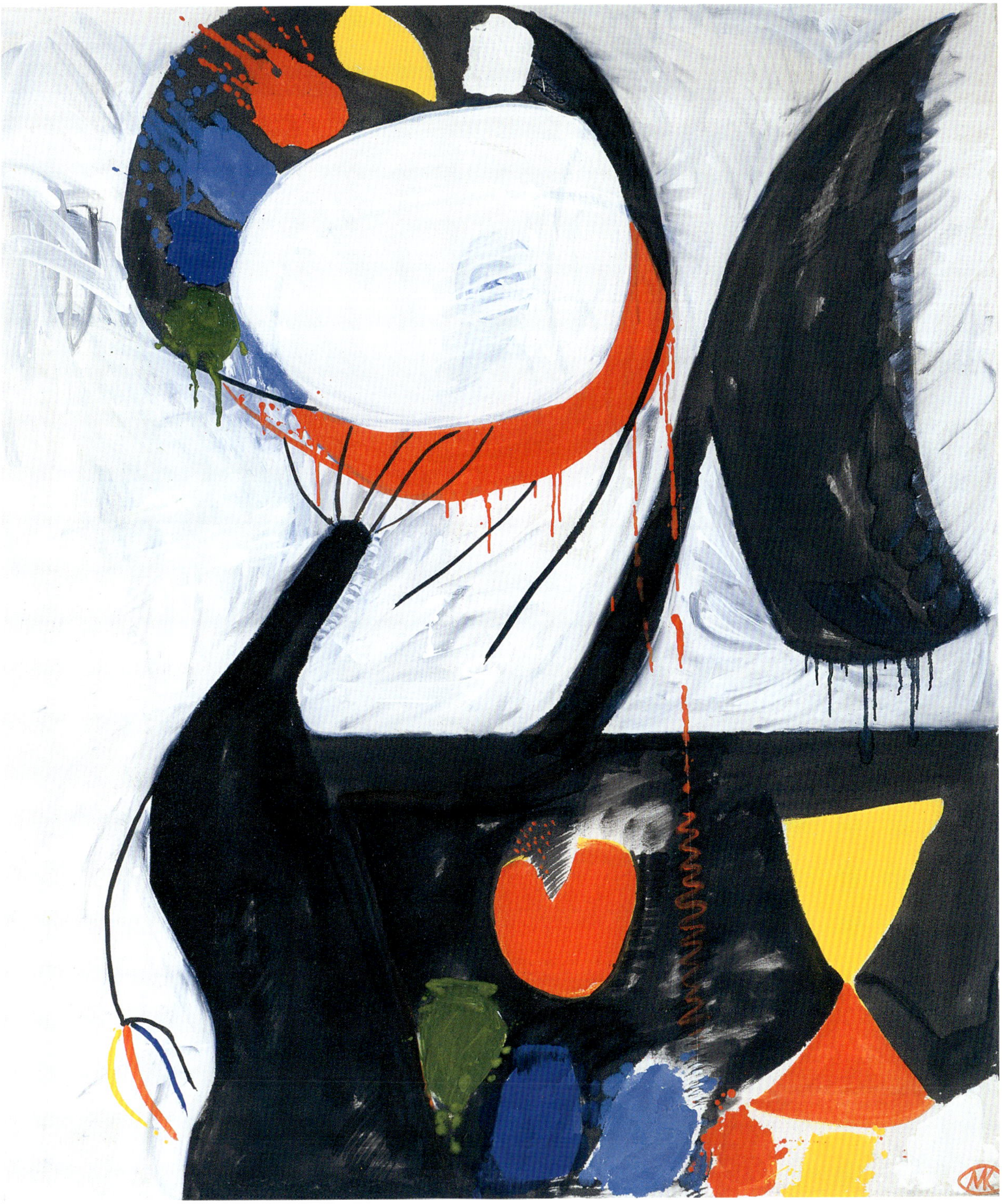

Марина Каверзина / Marina Kaverzina

Троица / The Trinity

2001, oil on canvas, 62 1/2 x 58 1/2 inches

(cat. no. 15)

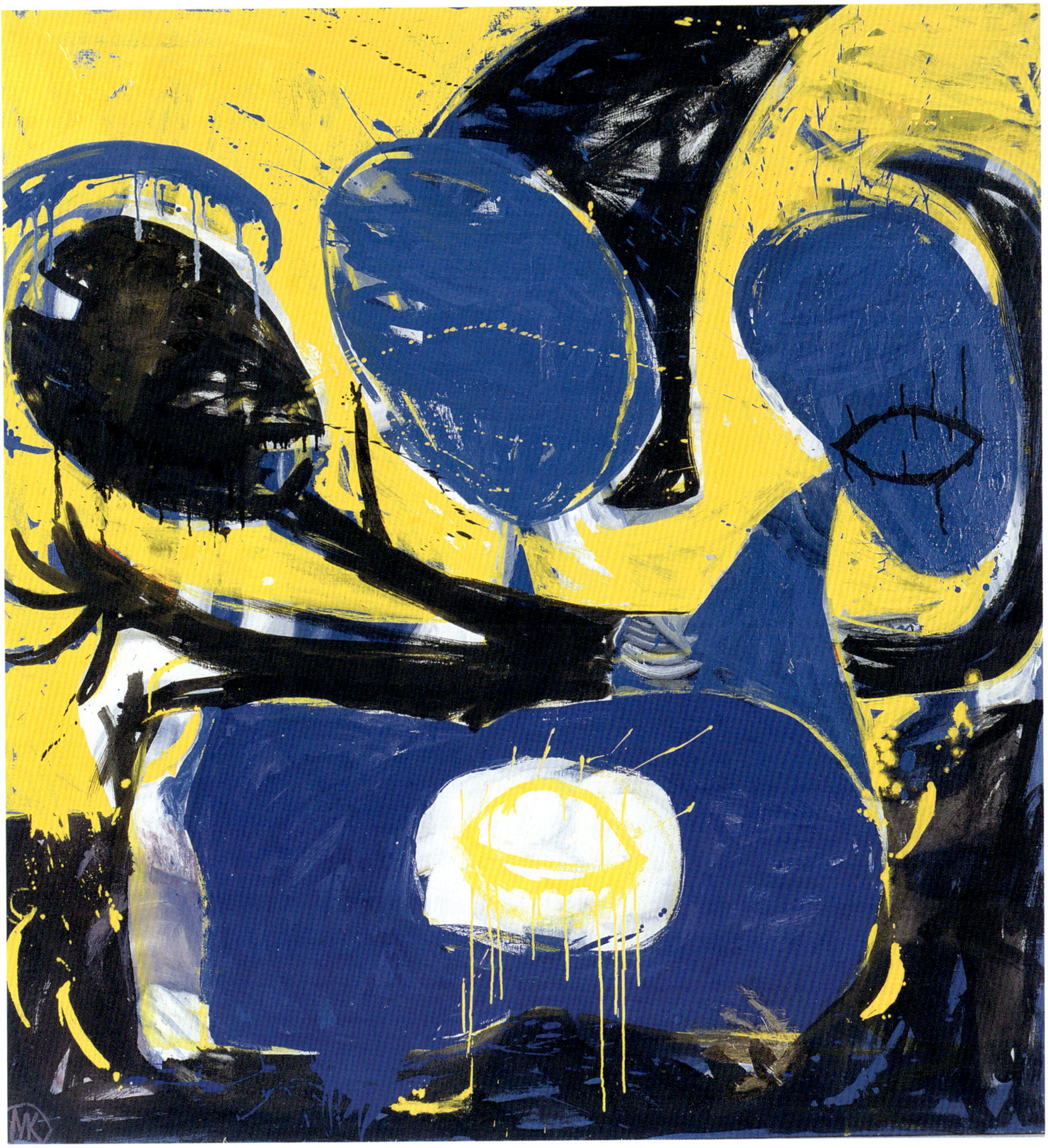

Александр Лоцман
Aleksandr Lotsman

Люблю тоскливое пространство полей, ждущих зимы. Засохшие одинокие стебли Травы в зимнем поле. Умершее чудо, которое обновится весной. Далекие горизонты сентябрьского неба. Умиротворение и покой этих дней. Люблю ожидание пьянящего, солнечного тепла в апреле.

Все это так бесконечно, так маняще. . .

I love the maudlin space of fields awaiting winter. The dry lonely blades of grass in a winter field. The passing miracle that is renewed by spring. The distant horizons of a September sky. The peacefulness and calm of these days. I love the expectation of the intoxicating warmth of the sun in April.

All of this so eternal, so enticing. . .

Александр Лоцман / Aleksandr Lotsman

Птицы / Birds

2000, oil on canvas, 28 1/2 x 39 inches

(cat. no. 16)

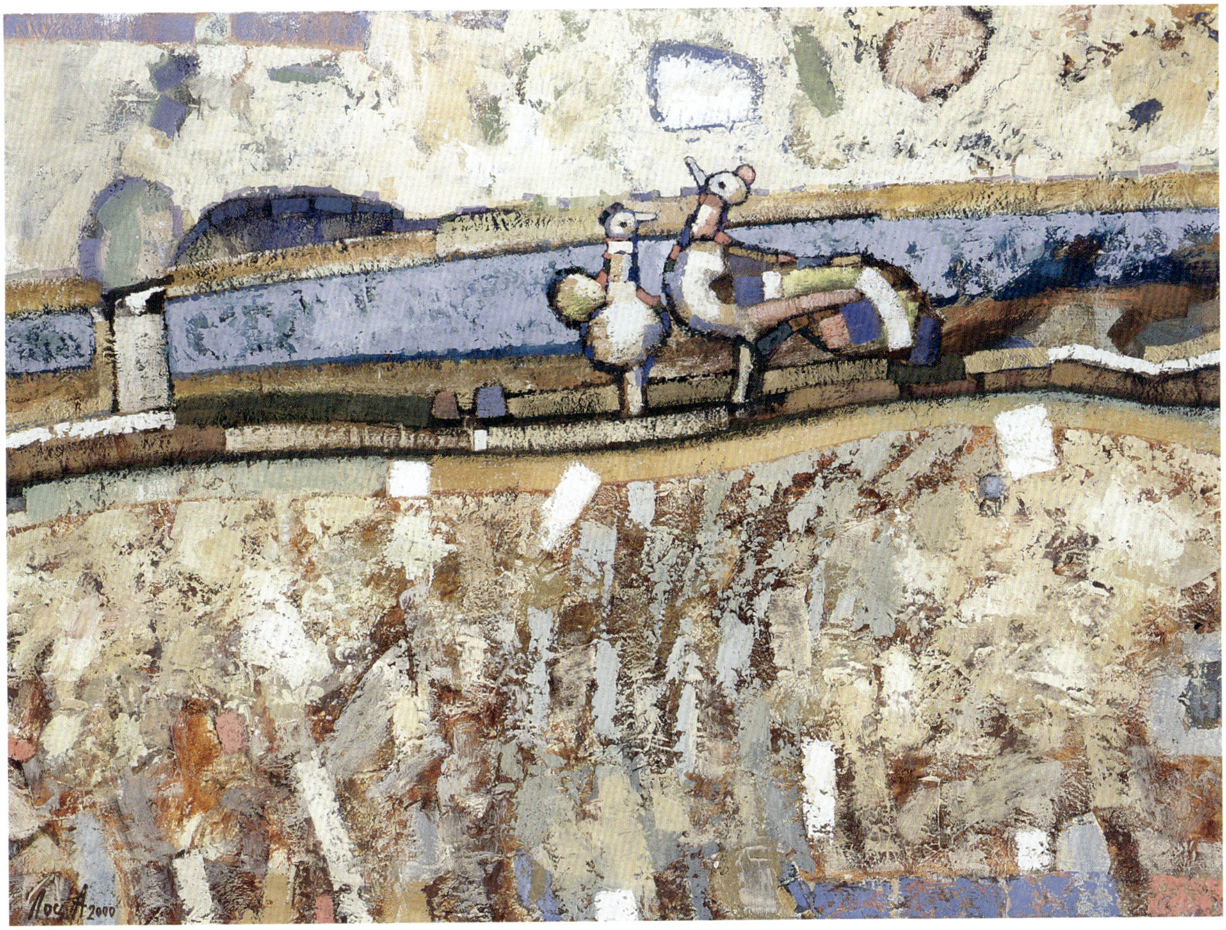

Александр Лоцман / Aleksandr Lotsman

Вечерние травы / Evening Weeds

2001, oil on canvas, 39 x 31 1/2 inches

(cat. no. 18)

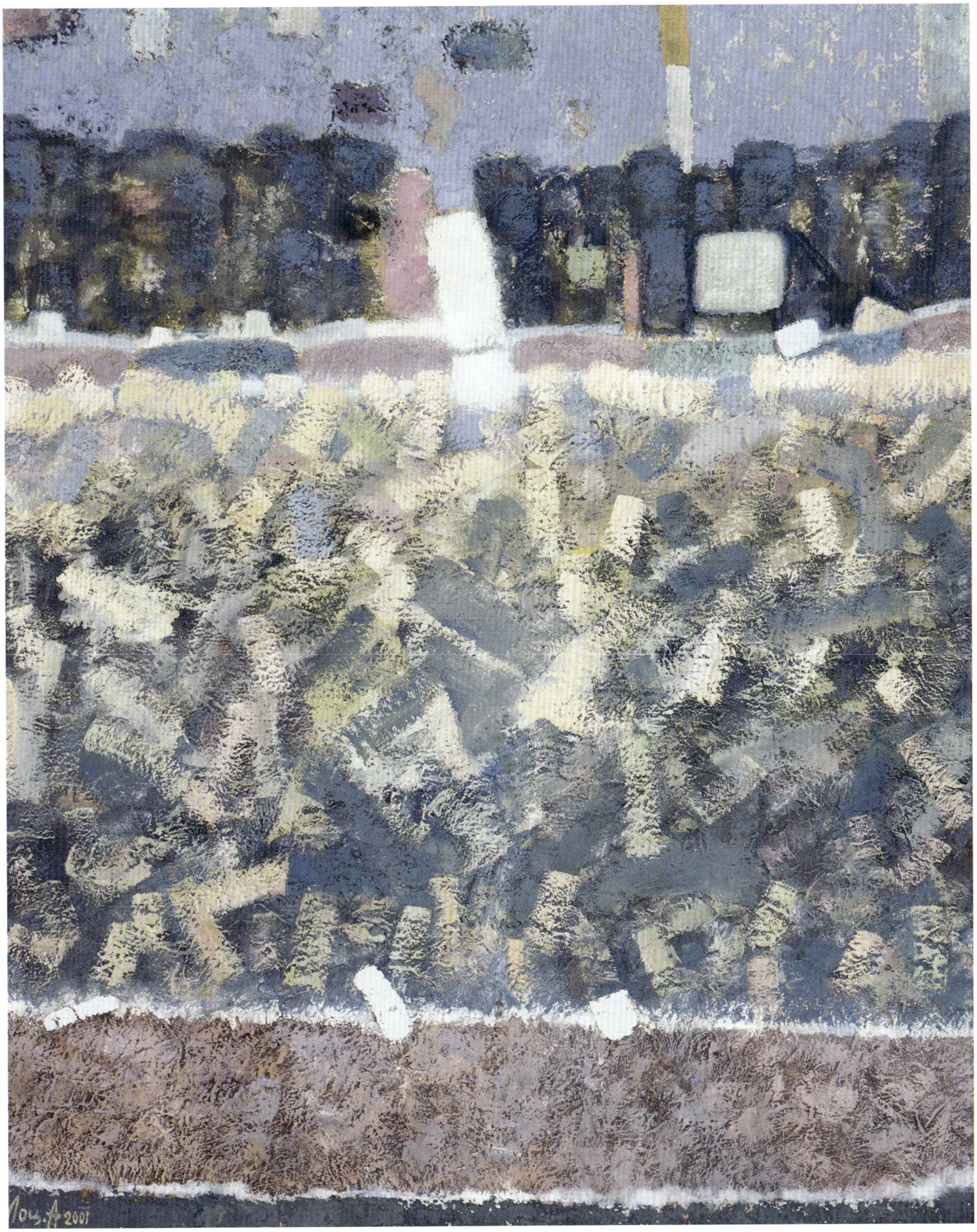
2001

Александр Лоцман / Aleksandr Lotsman

Дом под деревом / A House under a Tree

2001, oil on canvas, 39 x 28 1/2 inches

(cat. no. 19)

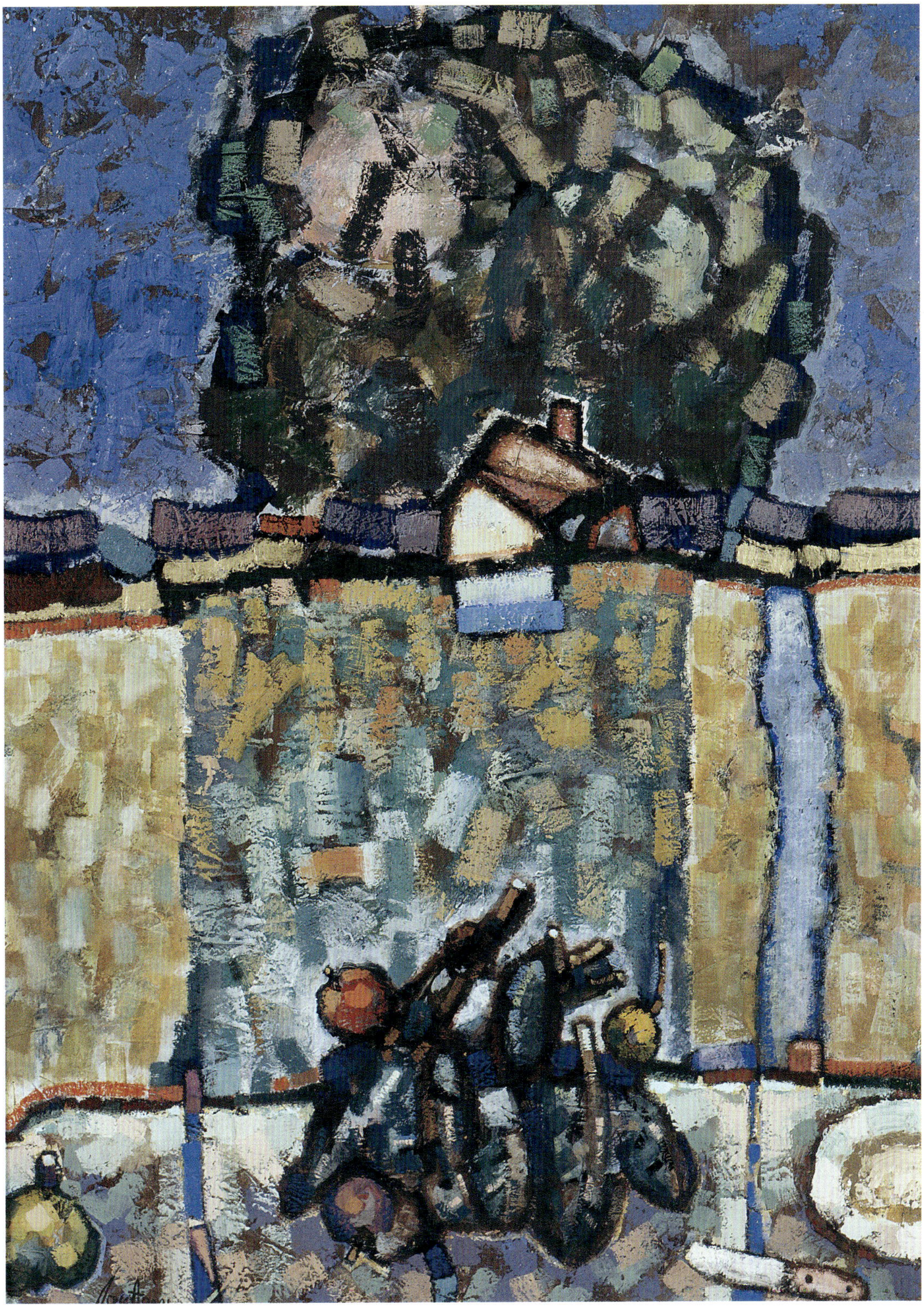

Евгений Орлов
Evgeny Orlov

. . . извлечь предметы из пространства,
растворить их в пространстве,
сделать предметы сущностью пространства,
а сущностью пространства определить в нем место человека,
через человека создать состояние пространства

. . . to coax objects from space,
to dissolve them in space,
to make objects the essence of space,
to define in that space the place of humankind,
to create through humankind the condition of space

Евгений Орлов / Evgeny Orlov

Окно / A Window

1992, oil on canvas, 52 1/2 x 66 1/4 inches

(cat. no. 21)

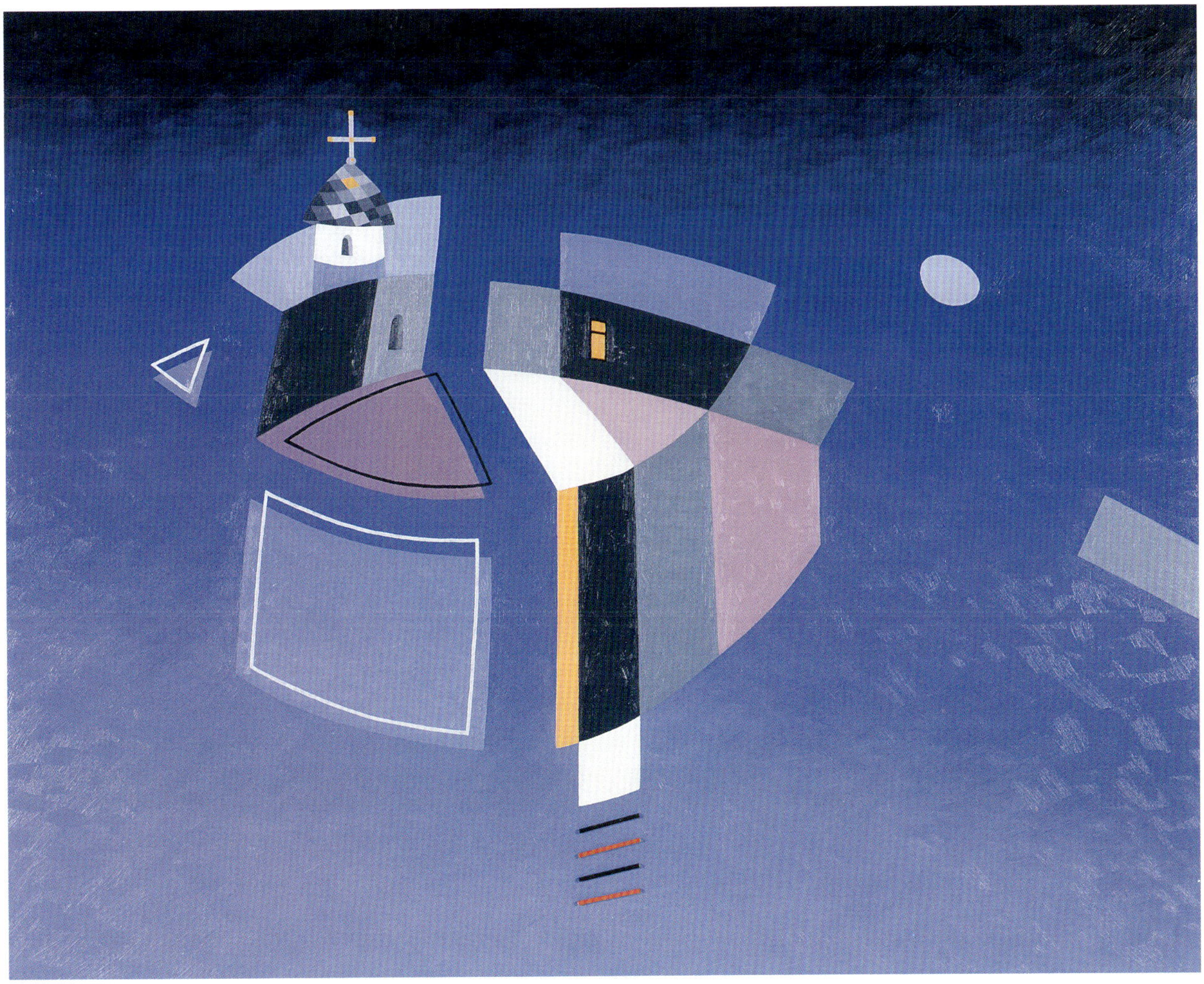

Евгений Орлов / Evgeny Orlov

Старая Деревня / An Old Village

1995, oil on canvas, 52 1/2 x 66 1/4 inches

(cat. no. 27)

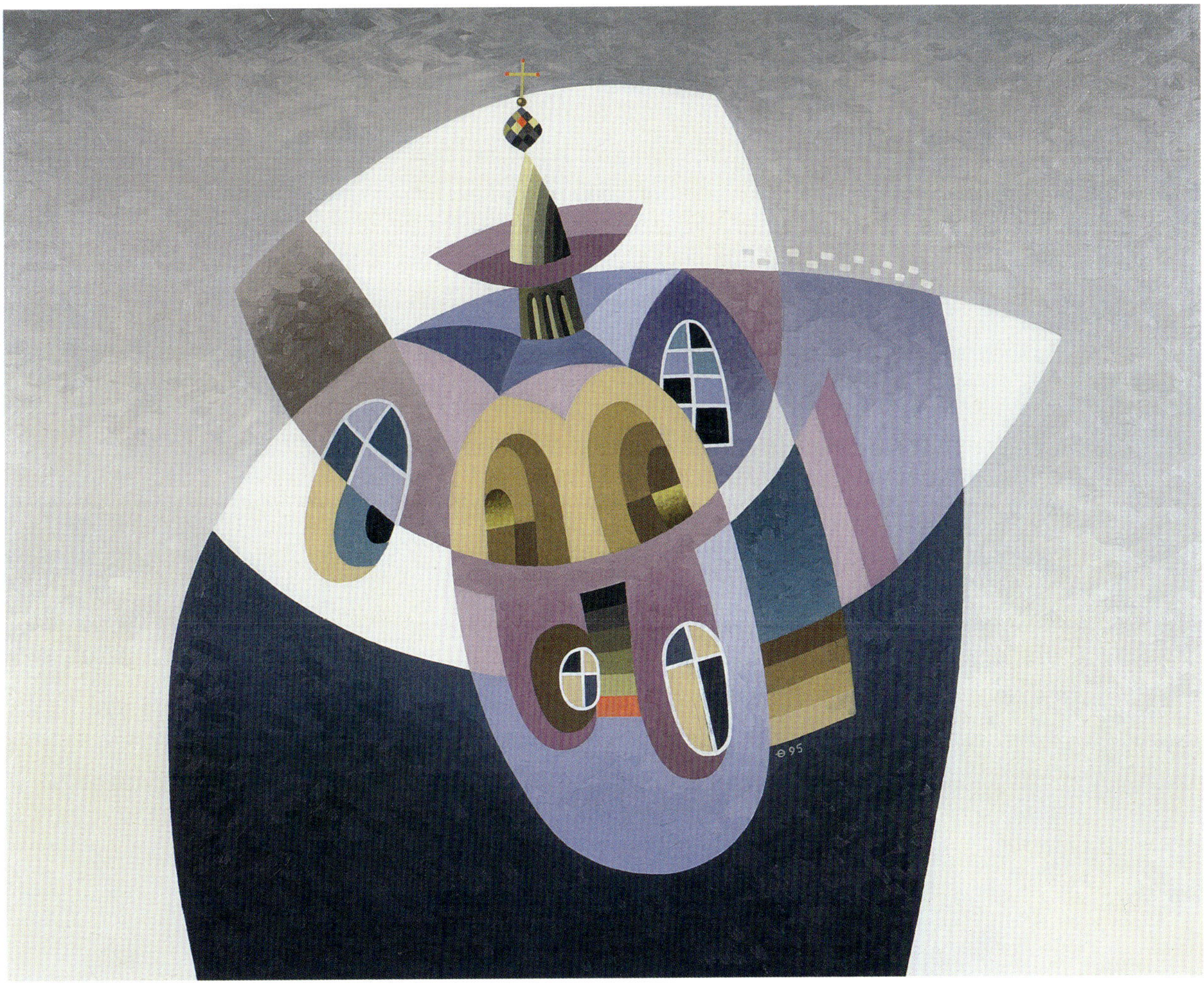

Евгений Орлов / Evgeny Orlov

Белый город / Bely Gorod

1996, oil on canvas, 47 x 29 inches

(cat. no. 31)

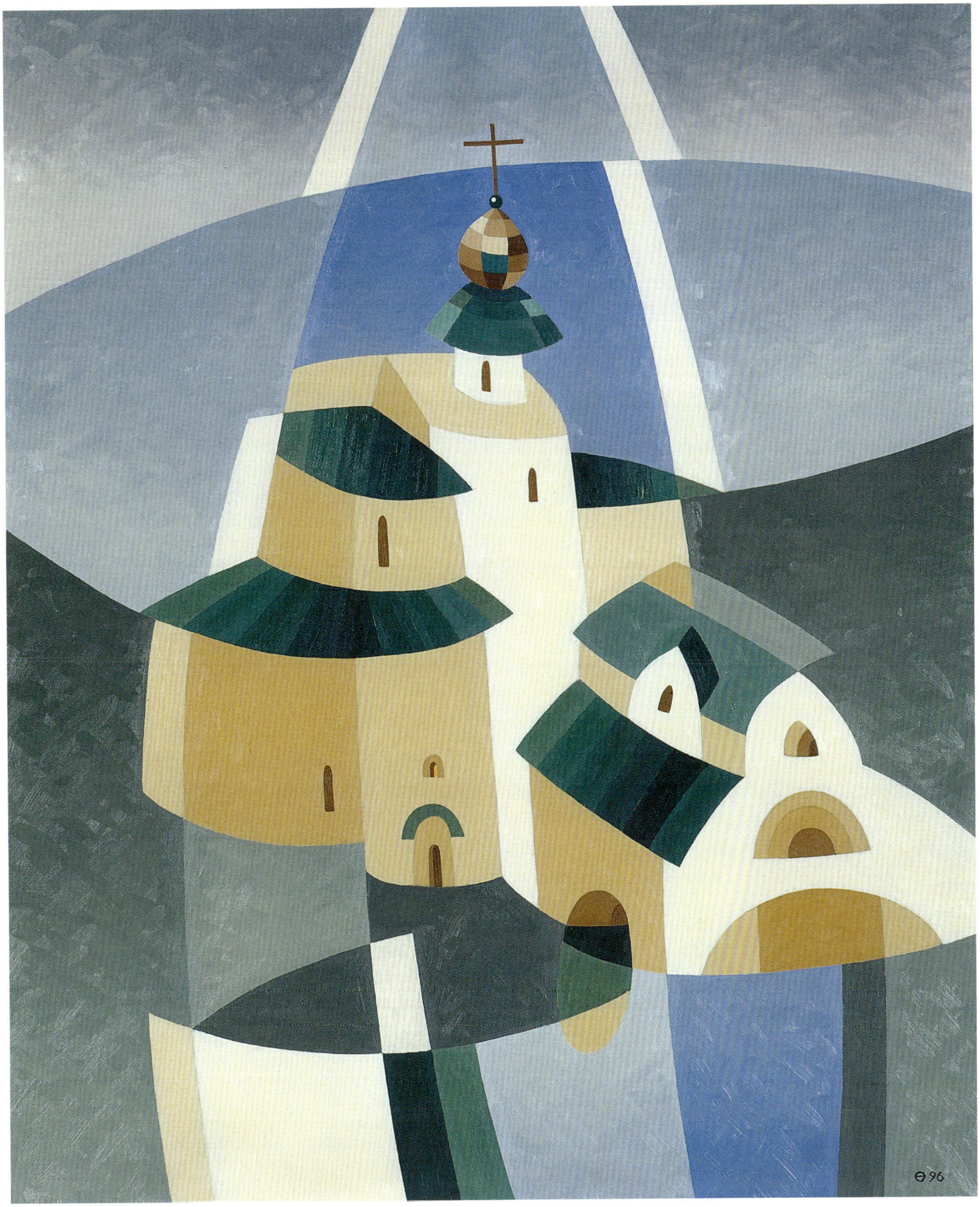

Игорь Орлов
Igor Orlov

В моем творчестве я стремлюсь не к созданию отдельных произведений, но единого силового поля, в пространстве которого открывается путь в мир образов.

Чаще всего это имеет характер вспышек, в которых на мгновение высвечивается какой-то удар или орнамент.

In my creative work I aspire to the creation not of individual works of art, but of a single field of strength, in the space of which is revealed a path into the world of images.

More often than not this has the character of flashes, in which momentarily some kind of stroke or embellishment lights up.

Игорь Орлов / Igor Orlov

Всю ночь пили испанское вино / We Drank Spanish Wine all Night

1997, oil on canvas, 62 1/2 x 50 3/4 inches

(cat. no. 33)

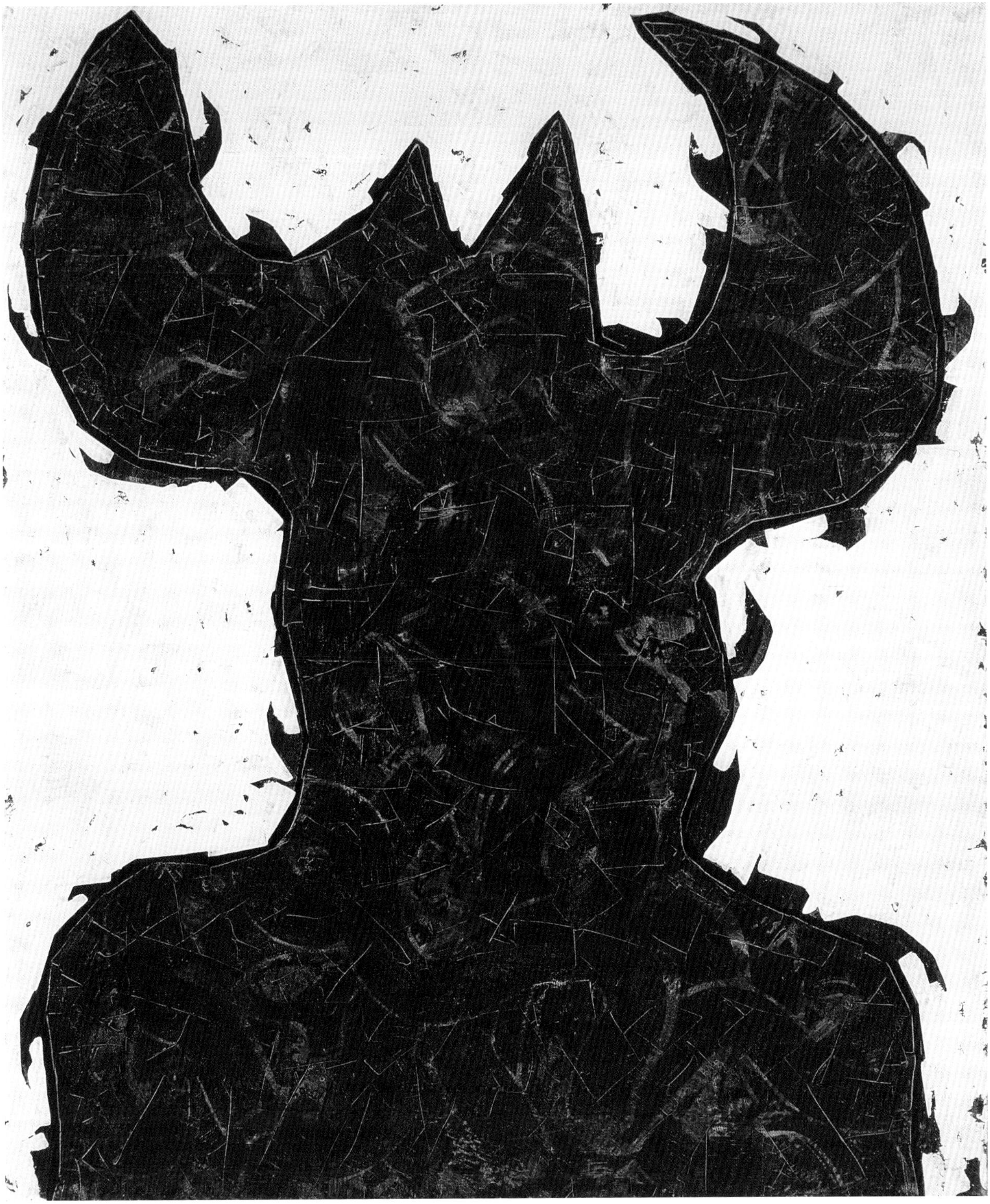

Игорь Орлов / Igor Orlov

Знаки / Signs

2001, tempera on canvas, 39 x 82 inches

(cat. no. 35)

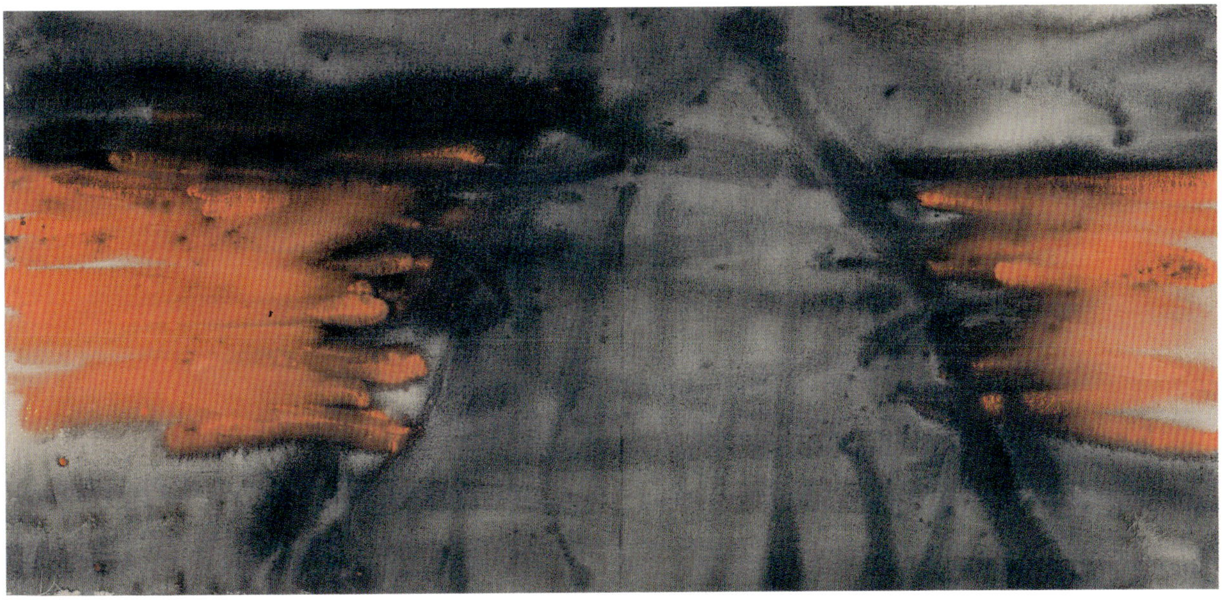

Игорь Орлов / Igor Orlov

Без Названия / Untitled

2001, tempera on canvas, 46 1/4 x 66 inches

(cat. no. 36)

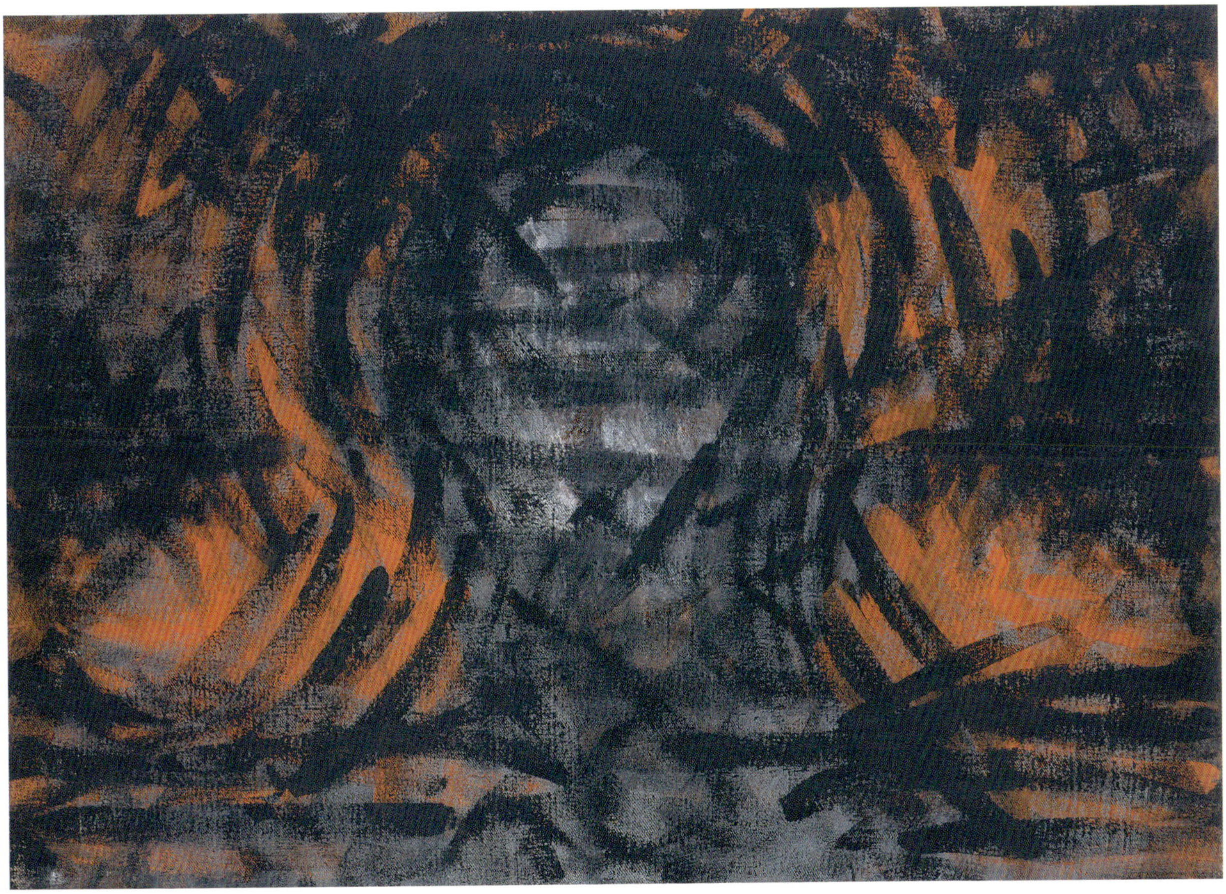

Светлана Цвиркунова
Svetlana Tsvirkunova

«Одни рисуют земное с чувством, другие заменяют его абстракцией, но счастливы, сочетающие силу абстракции с экономной мерой чувства. Тогда гармония», — это слова Владимира Стерлигова стали девизом моего творчества.

Владимир Стерлигов (1904-1973), ученик Казимира Малевича, продолжал традиции ГИНХУКа (Государственного института художественной культуры), существовавшего в Петрограде в начале 1920-х годов.

"Some draw the earthly with feeling, others exchange it for abstraction, but the fortunate ones are those, who combine the force of abstraction with just the right touch of feeling. Then you have harmony." These are the words of Vladimir Sterlingov. They have become the motto of my creative work.

Vladimir Sterlingov (1904-1973), a pupil of Kazimir Malevich, continued the traditions of GINKhuKa (the State Institute of Artistic Culture) that existed in Petrograd at the beginning of the 1920s.

Светлана Цвиркунова / Svetlana Tsvirkunova

Купола / Cupola

2001, paper collage on canvas, 46 3/4 x 50 3/4 inches

(cat. no. 37)

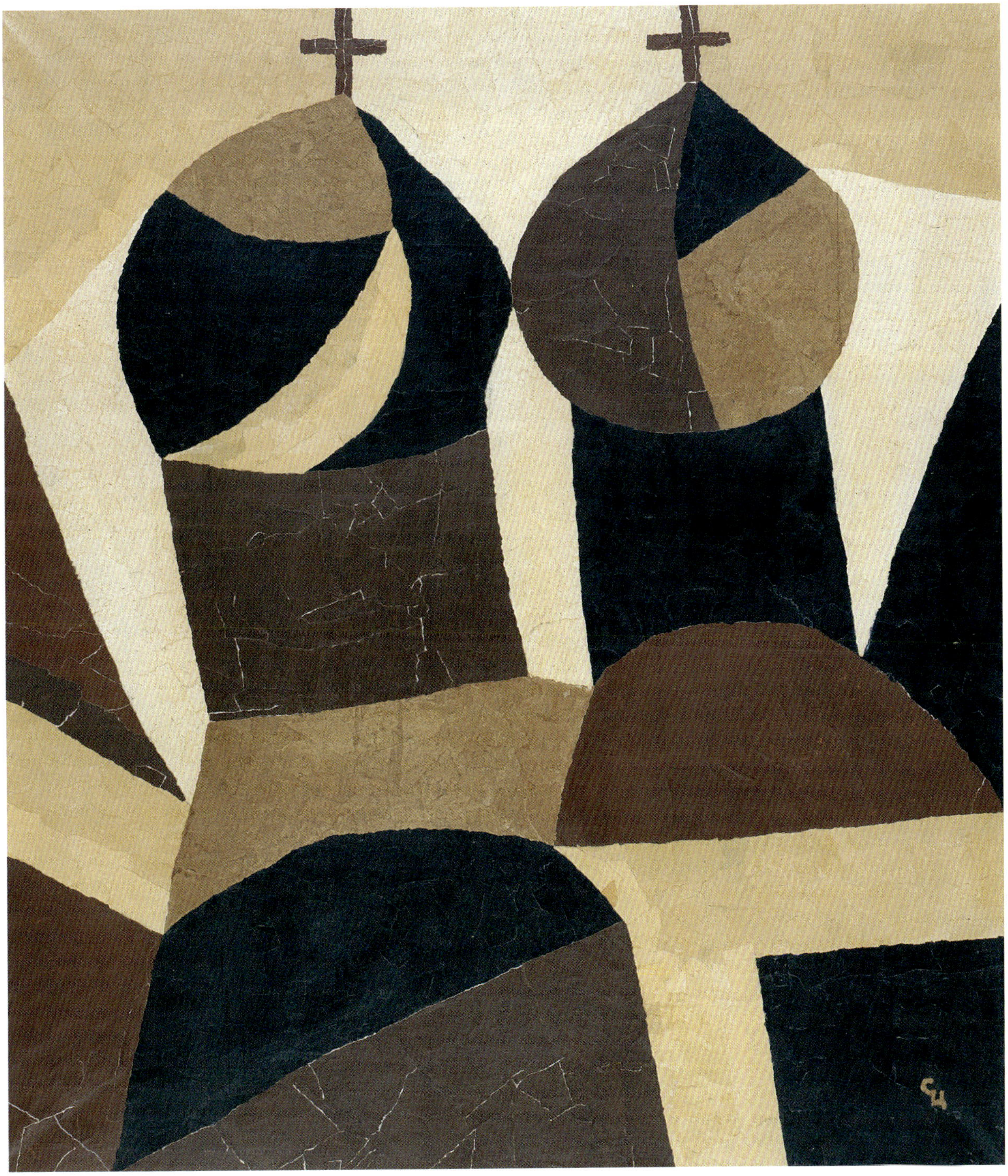

Светлана Цвиркунова / Svetlana Tsvirkunova

Женский портрет / Portrait of a Woman

2001, paper collage on canvas, 50 3/4 x 39 inches

(cat. no. 39)

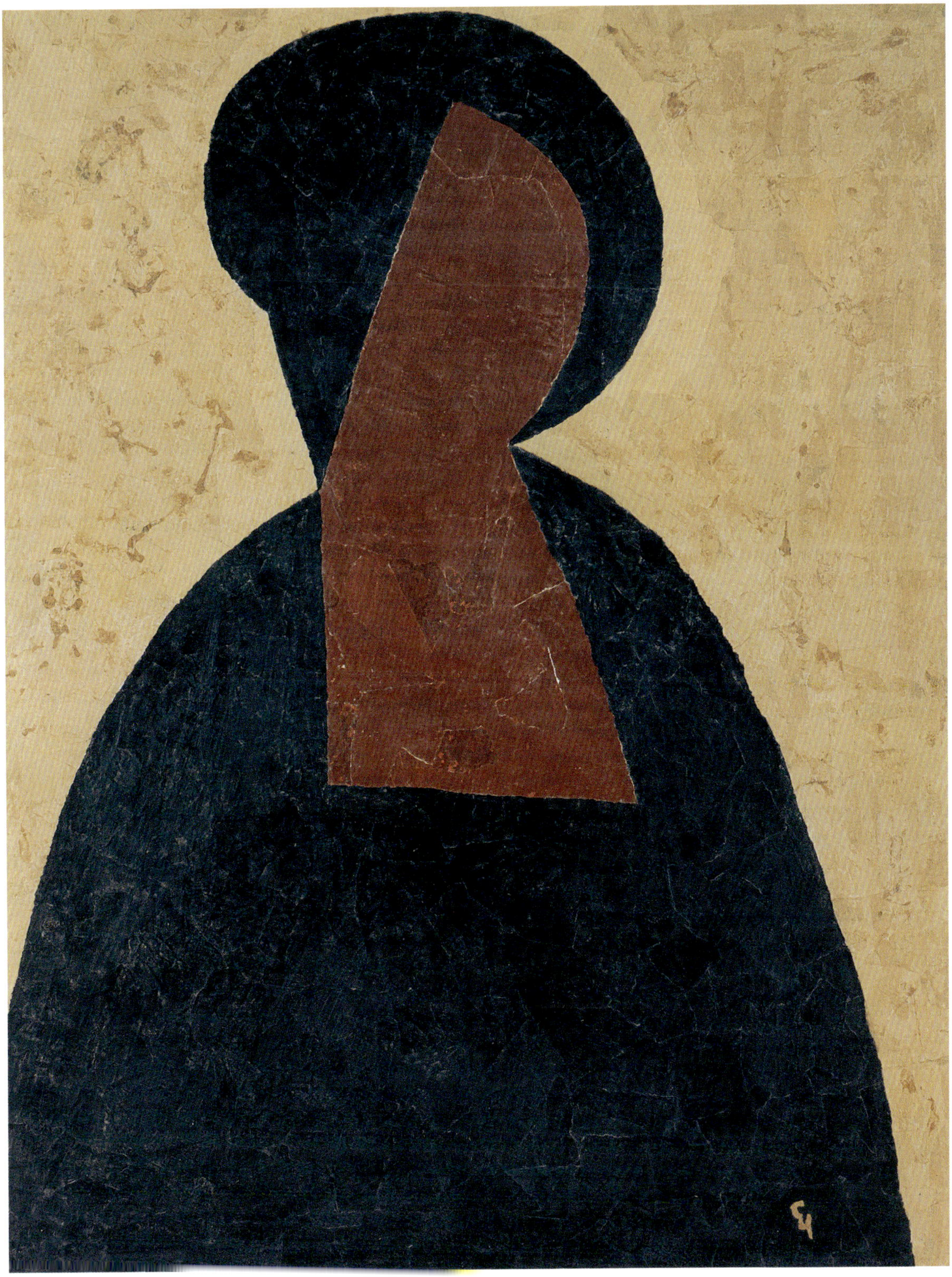

Светлана Цвиркунова / Svetlana Tsvirkunova

Натюрморт с яблоком / Still Life with an Apple

2001, paper collage on canvas, 46 3/4 x 50 3/4 inches

(cat. no. 40)

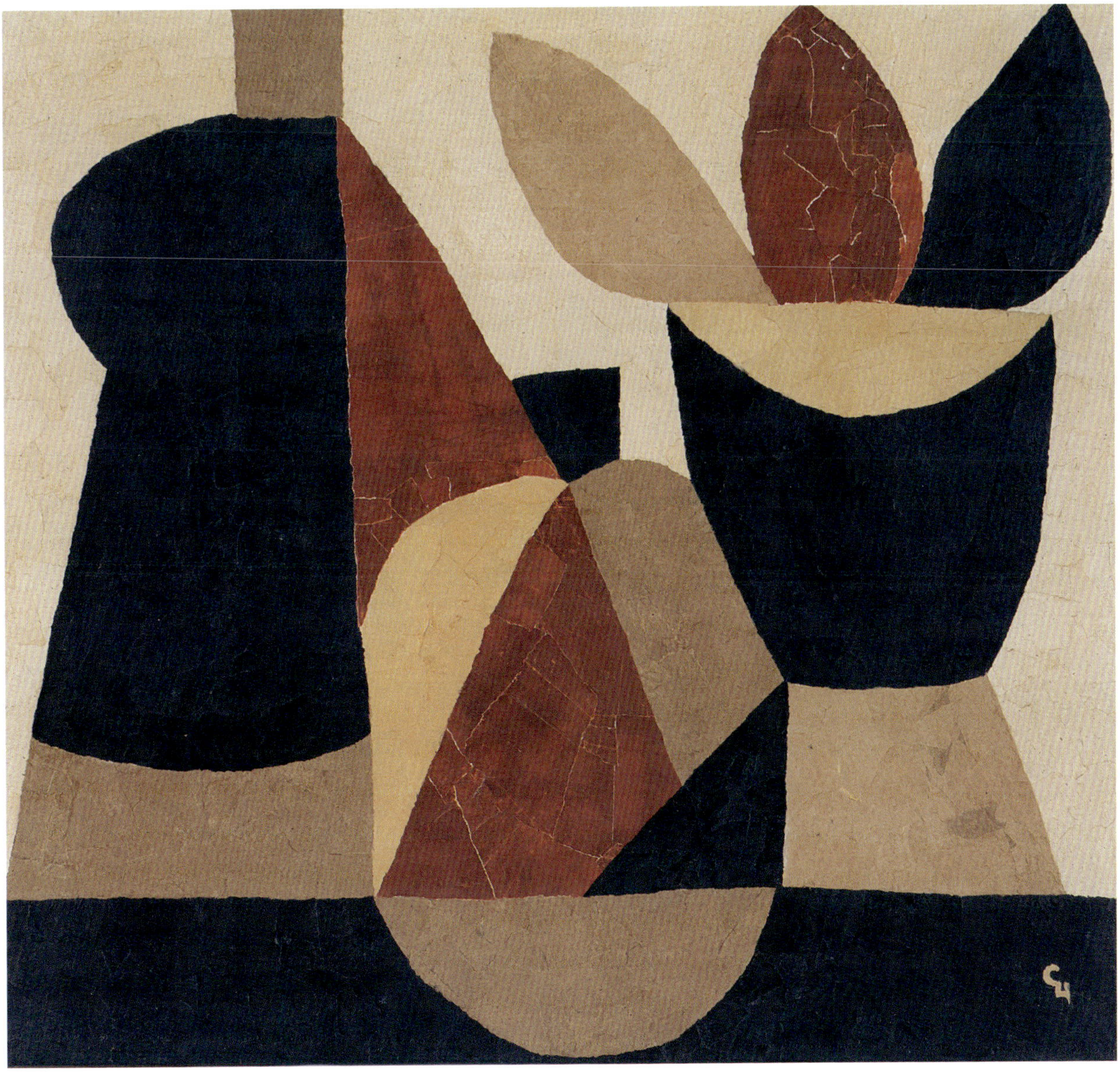

Виктор Андреев
Viktor Andreev

Viktor Andreev was born in the Ural Mountains of Russia in 1955. He graduated from art school in Sverdlovsk, Russia. Andreev moved to St. Petersburg in 1976 and graduated from the Repin Academy for Fine Arts in 1983. He has been a member of the artists' organization "The 5th Quarter" and the "Society for Free Culture" at Pushkinskaya 10 since 1992.

Since 1995 Andreev has been involved in pedagogical work as the head of a children's art studio. He is also the founder of a modern art studio at Pushkinskaya 10, which functions as an ongoing master class in modern art. Subjects taught there include drawing, art composition, and modern examples of art. The studio is open to students of all ages. His works have been exhibited in St. Petersburg and Moscow, Russia; Tallinn, Estonia; Riga, Latvia; Stockholm, Sweden; Finland; Lyon, France; Munich, Germany; Brazil; and New York City. He has works in the collections of The Museum of the History of St. Petersburg, Russia, and Riga City Museum, Latvia.

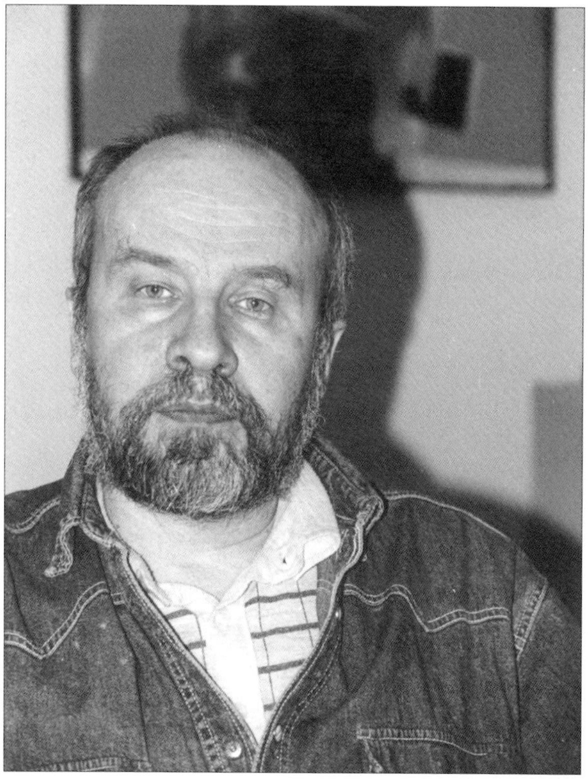

Виктор Андреев / Viktor Andreev

Алексей Чистяков
Alexei Chistyakov

Alexei Chistyakov was born in 1962 in St. Petersburg, Russia. He graduated from the Serov College of Art, then he studied at the Mukhina Academy of Art from 1984 until 1989. Chistyakov joined the State Association of Artists in 1992, and has been a member of the "Society for Free Culture" at Pushkinskaya 10 since 1990.

He has regularly participated in exhibitions both in Russia and abroad since 1982, and since 1999 his art has been presented on Sotheby's Internet Gallery. In St. Petersburg, he has had one-person exhibitions at Pushkinskaya 10's "21" Gallery (2000 and 2001) and "Art Polygon" Gallery(1999). Chistyakov has also had one-person exhibitions in Germany and England (1991) and the Central Art Gallery, Moscow, Russia (2001). He has been involved in many projects, including the Independent Film Festival of the Center for Cinema in St. Petersburg (1990), the "Rose of the World" project in Germany (1992), the "Back to the Future" project in St. Petersburg (1995), and the "STRIZH" project (Contemporary Technology in Russian Icon Painting) in St. Petersburg (2000).

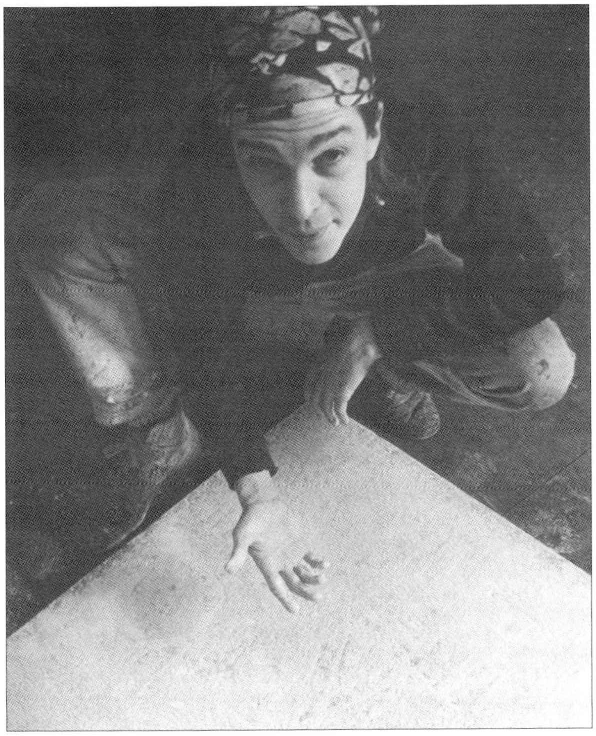

Алексей Чистяков / Alexei Chistyakov

Марина Каверзина
Marina Kaverzina

Marina Kaverzina was born in 1951 in St. Petersburg, Russia. She studied art history in Moscow, before beginning her creative work as an artist in painting, collage, graphic art, and theatrical design. She defines her work as "flying realism," the appeal of masses which have been transformed into forms.

Kaverzina has created several muti-media installations: "Over Fish and Under Birds" (Forms in Black Sound and Space) at the "21" Gallery at Pushkinskaya 10; "Figures From My Cosmos" in Nancy, France; and "Noisy Sphere #2" (Iron and Sound in Space) at "21" Gallery. Since 1983 she has participated in numerous exhibitions and art festivals in Russia, Latvia, Spain, France, Germany, Austria, Finland, and Denmark. She has been a member of the "Society for Free Culture" at Pushkinskaya 10 since 1992. She hopes to complete her current projects "The Utilization of Unrealized Women's Sexuality for Peaceful Aims" and "The Transformation of Iron Wastes into Objects of Culture" in the coming year.

Александр Лоцман
Aleksandr Lotsman

Born 1947 in St. Petersburg, Russia, Aleksandr Lotsman developed as an artist in the 1980s. He has been a regular participant in many exhibitions held by "The Fellowship for Experimental Fine Arts" in St. Petersburg, Russia. In the 1980s and 1990s he participated in exhibitions in Riga and Tallinn, Estonia; Hamburg, Bonn, and Erfurt, Germany; Paris, France; and San Diego, California.

His paintings are in the collections of The Museum of the History of St. Petersburg, The Museum of Valaam Monastery, and The Historical Museum of Omsk, all in Russia. His works are in many private collections in St. Petersburg and Moscow, as well as in Sweden, Germany, France, and the United States. He is a member of the International Federation of Artists of UNESCO, and since the 1990s he has been a member of the "Free Culture Society" at Pushkinskaya 10. He presently teaches creative art.

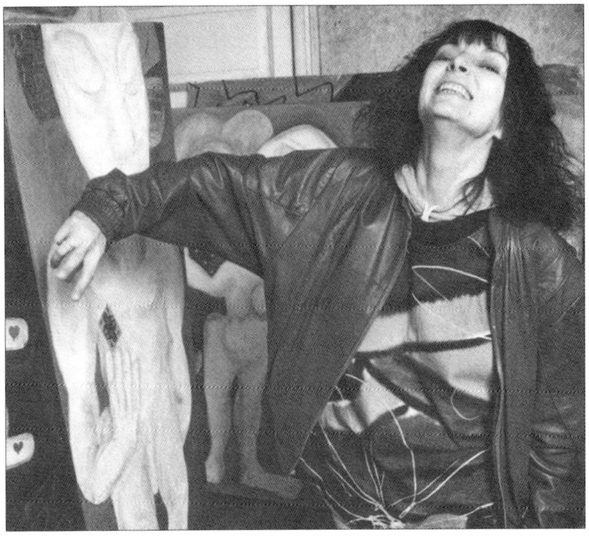

Марина Каверзина / Marina Kaverzina

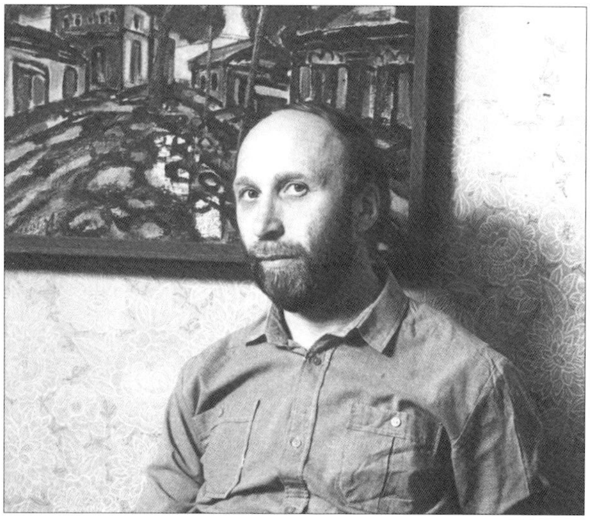

Александр Лоцман / Aleksandr Lotsman

Евгений Орлов
Evgeny Orlov

Evgeny Orlov was born in 1952 in St. Petersburg, Russia. He attended both Nautical School and the Art Academy of St. Petersburg, where he graduated in 1974. From 1976 until 1977 he trained in abstract composition with Nicholai Sychev.

In 1977, Orlov became the art director for the Sokol Construction Company and served in that capacity until 1989. In 1980 he began to paint religious subjects, beginning with the Russian Orthodox churches of the Pskov region of Russia. In 1983 he helped to organize the "underground" artists of Leningrad and to hold exhibitions with other artists called "The Partnership for Experimental Art." In 1987 he organized the first exhibition dedicated to the millennium of Russian Orthodoxy. Since then, he has been a participant in numerous art exhibitions not only in Russia but also abroad. He is the chief consultant of the Terseus Gallery in Stockholm, Sweden, which specializes in contemporary Russian art. He is also vice-president of the "Society for Free Culture" at Pushkinskaya 10 and one of the founders of the artists' organizations entitled "The Fifth Quarter" and "The Seven." Orlov is the director and vice president of The Museum for Nonconformist Art at the Cultural Arts Center of Pushkinskaya 10.

His one-person exhibitions include the N.K. Roerich Museum, Isvara, Russia (1986); the "Five Corners" Exhibition Hall, St. Petersburg (1987); the Terseus Gallery, Stockholm, Sweden (1990, 1991, 1992, 1994, 1996, 1998, 2000); the Fedor Gallery (1993), the Palitra Gallery (1995), The Museum of the History of St. Petersburg (1996), the Center for International Business (1997), and the Manege Central Exhibition Hall (2001), all in St. Petersburg, Russia. His work is in many public collections, including the Manege Central Exhibition Hall, The State Russian Museum, the Diagalev Center for Contemporary Art, all St. Petersburg, Russia; the Museum of Valaam Monastery, Karelia, Russia; the Gleser Collection, Moscow, Russia; the Terseus Gallery and the State Cultural Institution, Stockholm, Sweden; and the Zimmerli Art Museum, Rutgers University, New Jersey. He also has works in private collections in New York, Chicago, Los Angeles, San Francisco, and Washington, DC.

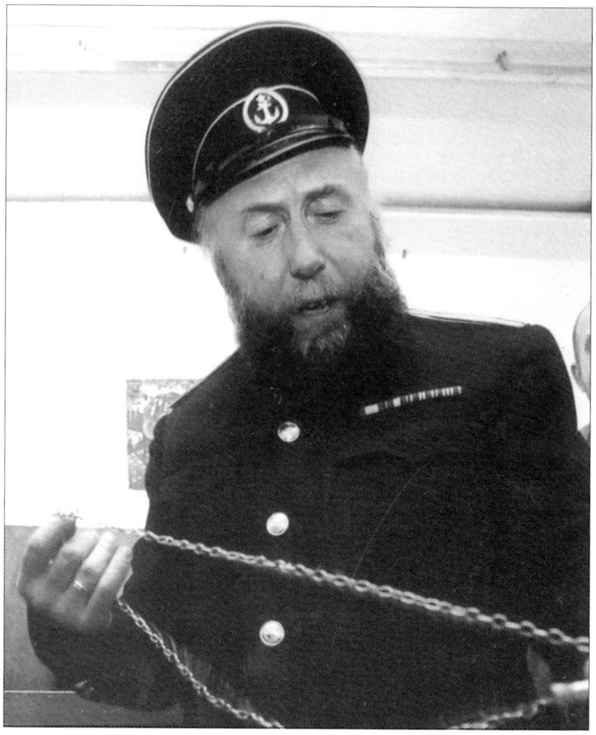

Евгений Орлов / Evgeny Orlov

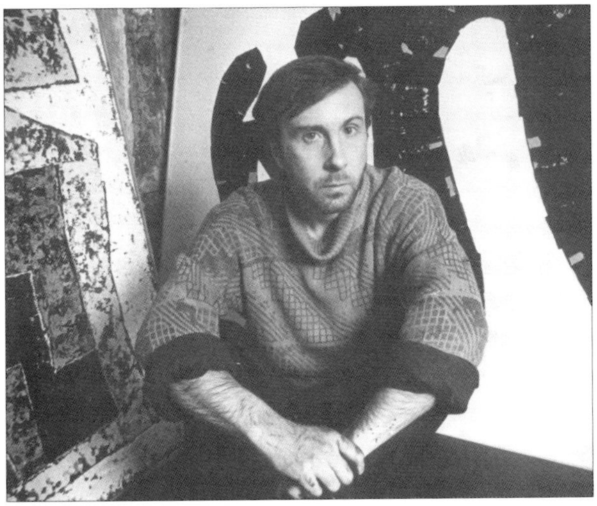

Игорь Орлов / Igor Orlov

Игорь Орлов
Igor Orlov

Igor Orlov was born in 1959 in St. Petersburg, Russia. His creative work began in 1977, when he received private tutoring in art at the studio of Nicholai Sychev. Since 1984, he has been a member of the Fellowship of Experimental Visual Artists, and since 1989 he has been an active member of the "Society for Free Culture" at Pushkinskaya 10. He has studied oriental art and philosophy, as well as music philosophy. In 1995 Orlov founded a studio and school for "automatic drawing."

His one-person exhibitions include the Manege Central Exhibition Hall (1992, 1997), the Navicula Art Gallery (1993), the "21" Gallery at Pushkinskaya 10, all St. Petersburg, Russia; the Center for Contemporary Art (1998), Warsaw, Poland; and the Tabaksfabrikken Cultural Center (1999), Esbjerg, Denmark. His works in public collections include the Museum of Valaam Monastery, Karelia, Russia; the Diagalev Center for Art and the Manege Central Exhibition Hall, both in St. Petersburg, Russia; the Narva Museum, Narva, Estonia; the Zimmerli Art Museum, Rutgers University, New Jersey; and the Fisher Gallery, Los Angeles, California.

Светлана Цвиркунова
Svetlana Tsvirkunova

Svetlana Tsvirkunova was born in St. Petersburg, Russia, in 1968. She began studying art in 1997 in Gennady Zyubov's studio and became acquainted with the ideas of the Russian avant-garde school of art. She joined the young artist's organization "OKNO" in 1997, and in 1998 became a member of "The 17th of April," a group of artists brought together by Zyubov. In 2000 she became a member of the St. Petersburg Creative Artists Collective as well as the art research group "Form + Color." She has been a member of the "Society of Free Culture" at Pushkinskaya 10 since 2001.

She has had exhibitions at the S.P.A.S. Gallery (1997, 1998, 1999, 2001), the "Art Polygon" Gallery (2000) and The Museum of Nonconformist Art (2001) at Pushkinskaya 10, the Manege Central Exhibition Hall (2000, 2001), the St. Petersburg Creative Artists Gallery (2000), the Anichkov Palace (2001), all in St. Petersburg, Russia; and the Aurora Gallery (2000), Tver, Russia. Her works in public collections include The Museum of Modern Art, Kemerovo, Russia; The Museum of Nonconformist Art at Pushkinskaya 10, the St. Petersburg Creative Artists Collection, the S.P.A.S. Gallery, all in St. Petersburg, Russia; and The Museum of Modern Ecclesiastical Art, Sviato-Troitsky Nunnery, Kolomna, Russia.

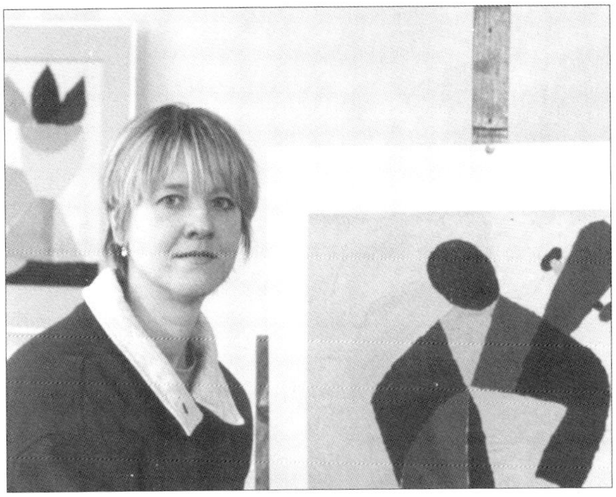

Светлана Цвиркунова / Svetlana Tsvirkunova

CHECKLIST OF THE EXHIBITION

Dimensions are given in inches, height precedes width. All the paintings are lent courtesy of the artists through arrangements with The Museum of Nonconformist Art, Pushkinskaya 10, St. Petersburg, Russia.

Виктор Андреев / Viktor Andreev
(born 1955, Ural Mountains, Russia)

1. *Композиция / Composition*
   2001, acrylic and lacquer on canvas,
   39 x 46 3/4 (illustrated, page 25)

2. *Композиция / Composition*
   2001, acrylic and lacquer on canvas,
   39 x 46 3/4

3. *Композиция / Composition*
   2001, acrylic and lacquer on canvas,
   39 x 45 (illustrated, page 27)

4. *Композиция / Composition*
   2001, acrylic and lacquer on canvas,
   39 x 46 3/4 (illustrated, page 29)

5. *Композиция / Composition*
   2001, acrylic and lacquer on canvas, 39 x 47

Алексей Чистяков / Alexei Chistyakov
(born 1962, St. Petersburg, Russia)

6. *Без Названия / Untitled*
   1994-97, oil on canvas, 64 1/4 x 59
   (illustrated, page 31)

7. *Без Названия / Untitled*
   1994-97, oil on canvas, 64 1/4 x 59

8. *Без Названия / Untitled*
   1999, oil on canvas, 27 1/4 x 54 1/2
   (illustrated, page 33)

9. *Без Названия / Untitled*
   1999, oil on canvas, 55 1/2 x 36 1/4
   (illustrated, page 35)

10. *Без Названия / Untitled*
    2000, oil on canvas, 55 1/2 x 36 1/4

Марина Каверзина / Marina Kaverzina
(born 1951, St. Petersburg, Russia)

11. *Голгофа / Golgotha*
    2001, oil on canvas, 62 1/2 x 58 1/2

12. *Пианист / A Pianist*
    2001, oil on canvas, 54 1/2 x 46 3/4
    (illustrated, page 37)

13. *Автопортрет / Self-Portrait*
    2001, oil on canvas, 54 1/2 x 46 3/4
    (illustrated, page 39)

14. *Испания / Spain*
    2001, oil on canvas, 54 1/2 x 46 3/4

15. *Троица / The Trinity*
    2001, oil on canvas, 62 1/2 x 58 1/2
    (illustrated, page 41)

Александр Лоцман / Aleksandr Lotsman
(born 1947, St. Petersburg, Russia)

16. *Птицы / Birds*
    2000, oil on canvas, 28 1/2 x 39
    (illustrated, page 43)

17. *Край поля / The Edge of a Field*
    2001, oil on canvas, 39 x 50 3/4

18. *Вечерние травы / Evening Weeds*
    2001, oil on canvas, 39 x 31 1/2
    (illustrated, page 45)

19. *Дом под деревом / A House under a Tree*
2001, oil on canvas, 39 x 28 1/2
(illustrated, page 47)

20. *Красный лес / A Red Forest*
2002, oil on canvas, 39 x 51 3/4

Евгений Орлов / Evgeny Orlov
(born 1952, St. Petersburg, Russia)

21. *Окно / A Window*
1992, oil on canvas, 52 1/2 x 66 1/4
(illustrated, page 49)

22. *Страна городов / A Country of Cities*
1993, oil on canvas, 56 1/2 x 68 1/4
(illustrated, page 6)

23. *Пространство креста / The Space of a Cross*
1993, oil on canvas, 56 1/2 x 45

24. *Волховские видения / Visions of Volkhov*
1993, oil with wood dowels and aluminum foil on canvas, 29 1/4 x 39

25. *Белый город / Bely Gorod*
1993, oil on canvas, 56 1/2 x 68 1/4

26. *Старая Ладога / Old Ladoga*
1994, oil with wood dowels and aluminum foil on canvas, 29 1/4 x 39

27. *Старая Деревня / An Old Village*
1995, oil on canvas, 52 1/2 x 66 1/4
(illustrated, page 51)

28. *Ковчег / The Ark*
1996, oil on canvas, diameter of 37 1/2
(illustrated, page 10 and cover)

29. *Летучий корабль / A Flying Ship*
1996, oil on canvas, diameter of 37 1/2

30. *На островах / On the Islands*
1996, oil on canvas, 47 x 39

31. *Белый город / Bely Gorod*
1996, oil on canvas, 47 x 29
(illustrated, page 53)

Игорь Орлов / Igor Orlov
(born 1959, St. Petersburg, Russia)

32. *Без Названия / Untitled*
1996, oil on canvas, 62 1/2 x 50 3/4

33. *Всю ночь пили испанское вино / We Drank Spanish Wine all Night*
1997, oil on canvas, 62 1/2 x 50 3/4
(illustrated, page 55)

34. *Композиция с двумя фигурами / Composition with Two Figures*
2001, tempera on canvas, 35 1/4 x 78

35. *Знаки / Signs*
2001, tempera on canvas, 39 x 82
(illustrated, page 57)

36. *Без Названия / Untitled*
2001, tempera on canvas, 46 1/4 x 66
(illustrated, page 59)

Светлана Цвиркунова / Svetlana Tsvirkunova
(born 1968, St. Petersburg, Russia)

37. *Купола / Cupola*
2001, paper collage on canvas, 46 3/4 x 50 3/4
(illustrated, page 61)

38. *Музыкант / Musician*
2001, paper collage on canvas, 58 1/2 x 50 3/4

39. *Женский портрет / Portrait of a Woman*
2001, paper collage on canvas, 50 3/4 x 39
(illustrated, page 63)

40. *Натюрморт с яблоком / Still Life with an Apple*
2001, paper collage on canvas, 46 3/4 x 50 3/4
(illustrated, page 65)

41. *Натюрморт с бутылкой / Still Life with a Bottle*
2001, paper collage on canvas, 50 3/4 x 46 3/4

"свободная культура"

ул. Пушкинская 10